Uniqueing Your Brand™

The Secret Chemistry behind Why Some Companies are Loved
and
How to Create Your Own Fiercely Loyal Customers
and Highly Profitable Business

Jeff Jochum

30

Me

The Rarest
Element

The Elemental Table of Brand Specialism

Discover　　Define　　Declare

101 **Un** Uniqueness	201 **Co** Competition	301 **Ch** Choices
102 **Si** Simplicity	202 **Po** Polarization	302 **In** Influence
103 **St** Stickiness	203 **Im** Imperfection	303 **Di** Discounts
104 **Be** Better	204 **Sg** Signatures	304 **Pr** Progress
105 **Qu** Quality	205 **Pe** Performance	305 **Se** Selling

Some Recommendations from Real People...

"There is a power in knowing who you are and what you want. It has made me a stronger businessperson and a much more self-aware woman. I went into this for help with my business, but the truth is it has improved me in all areas of my life. I am a better mom, wife, and friend. We associate happily ever after with fairy tales. Well, I can vouch for the fact that it's not a fairy tale at all... and that Jeff is my real-life knight in shining armor."
— Jennifer Rozenbaum, Owner, Jenerations.com

"I'll always remember what Jeff said to me very early on in our work together: 'My goal isn't to make you money; it's to make you happy.' Thinking about this, I realized that the end result of specializing isn't just about your business growing, becoming more successful, or making more money. (This idea aligns well with the advice I've always lived by.)"
— Brian Friedman, Professional Photographer, I Heart Radio Celebrity

"After several months of researching him, I wrote Jeff an e-mail. What followed over the next year transformed my life and continues to do so. With his directed guidance and tough-love questioning, I walked away from each meeting being mind-blown. The biggest power about specialism and knowing what makes me authentically unique is having the ability to articulate it and pass on those words to my clients, so they can pass them on to their friends and so forth. I feel so much clarity and focus now that I'm specialized about who I am and who my client is."
— Ivona Dixon, Small-Business Owner

"When your positioning is based on your purpose as a person, you learn that only you can be the best **you** for your client. I've discovered specialism isn't an ad campaign, sales promotion, or this year's marketing fad. It's a very real commitment to define the uniqueness of you, your business, and your purpose, and celebrate it in everything you say and do. Embrace it and it'll change your life, as it has mine.
— Jason Groupp, Director of Events, Emerald Expos

"The best part of Uniqueing Your Brand *is that it asks the right questions. And you'll find yourself getting better at questioning those answers, until you find the 'best' one, every time."*

— Christine Tremoulet, Author, Blogging Brilliantly for your Business

"I feel like I've completely rejuvenated my business, and I've never been more excited to set new goals, strategies, and tactics. Even if I fail with small experiments, which happens almost weekly, I am learning and growing from those failures, which are getting me closer to where I want to be. The people I've met and path I've traveled have been more fun and exciting than doing what I did when I pursued the same goals others were going after."
— Mike Larsen, Wedding Photographer

"In working with Jeff, my aim was to create focus and a business specialization that truly spoke to who I was as an individual. I learned that I am a dichotomy — which, in itself, is difficult to come to understand as a specialty. How can I be both one thing, and then an almost total opposite? The clarity for me came when I finally stepped back and looked at where I came from — my favorite place on earth: Pittsburgh. My city is a truly a city of dichotomy — cosmopolitan and country. Always new and leading with technology, yet country and homespun. I am my city, and my business is me."
— Leeann Marie, Entrepreneur and Pittsburg Evangelist

"After creating my own Authentically Unique Brand, my ideal clients doubled and so did my sales. I knew exactly whom I was trying to reach and what I was passionate about. Once I began declaring it, I didn't have to go out and search for my best customers. All I had to do was be myself. It truly is magical."
-Megan Bookhammer, small business owner

"In 2010, I went to a convention in Las Vegas and was walking through the lobby of Caesar's Palace with some friends when one of them stopped and said, 'Jeff Jochum is over there. You need to meet him.' I had heard of Jeff, as most people in my industry have, and I was thrilled to meet him. He gave me a big smile while shaking my

hand, and we talked for less than thirty seconds. But in those thirty seconds, what he said got to me. He was genuine, asking tough questions about my business, and I wanted more. Attending his workshop months later gave me my first taste of specialism and Authentically Unique Brands. Afterward, I started marketing **me**, *not just my general business concepts. The results were immediately great, and I knew I was on the right track. By following the chemistry defined in* Uniqueing Your Brand, *I learned to easily identify why I am truly unique, why people like me, and what made them want to spend their money with me. I'm now turning 'leads' into gold."*

— Tracy Moore, Community Businesswoman and Mom

"Be advised that the process isn't without pain, though for me it was certainly also full of laughter and created a renewed sense of purpose for my life. I was now able to be vocal, proud, and passionate about the things I believed in. I didn't have to hide behind any worry that I might offend someone or take a misstep. My passion draws in women whose values are closely aligned with mine, and working together is wonderful for both of us. Thanks to my Authentically Unique Brand, I began making small dents in the individual lives of businesses and have even started making a larger splash. It's no longer enough for me to touch just a handful of entrepreneurs each month. I'm hungry for more, and I'm excited to find ways to bring my why out on a larger scale so that even more of them feel empowered during their journey to success."

— Stephanie Ostermann, Word Nerd and Content Genius

"I was burnt out and had fallen out of love with my business. I had to decide if I was going to quit or reinvent myself somehow, so I began researching Jeff and specialism in 2012 and jumped in, almost immediately. It has turned out to be the greatest investment in myself and my career (so far.) In 2013 I created my Authentically Unique Brand and have been attracting my ideal clients — while cultivating a community of like-minded people — ever since. My work is more fulfilling than I ever could have imagined." **-Sarah Lehberger, SheWillThrive.com**

"I got to know Jeff a decade before I started working with him. I finally reached out because my company and I were at a crisis crossroads and needed to figure out who we were and why we were doing what we do, before we could move beyond it. I never could've imagined the newfound passion and purpose we all feel now, and I'm so grateful for it. Before we experienced this clarity, we were just spinning our wheels. We would get traction from time to time and inch forward, but it took so much effort, and every year burn out was predictable. Now everything is different. We make decisions faster. We are growing in our gifts, and we are doing our best to serve those around us… and encouraging them to serve others, as well. And on top of that, business is up 500 percent already this year!"
— David Jay, Serial Entrepreneur, CEO of Agree.com

"Specialism has given me very precise direction with my business. And with that gift of clarity, I am able to remain true to my uniqueness. And, that is what any entrepreneur calls priceless!"
-Michelle Ocampo, Global business entrepreneur

JEFF JOCHUM

UNIQUEING
—————— YOUR ——————
BRAND ™

THE **SECRET CHEMISTRY** BEHIND WHY
SOME COMPANIES ARE **LOVED**
——————— AND ———————
HOW TO CREATE YOUR **OWN** FIERCELY
LOYAL CUSTOMERS & HIGHLY
PROFITABLE BUSINESS

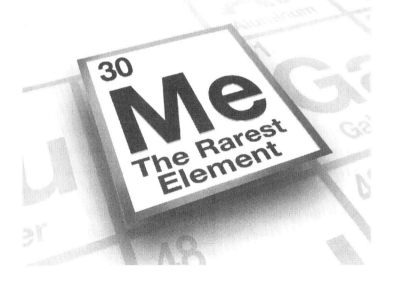

Uniqueing Your Brand

The Secret Chemistry behind Why Some Companies are Loved and How to Create Your Own Fiercely Loyal Customers and Highly Profitable Business

By Jeff Jochum

ISBN-13: 978-1523656981

ISBN-10: 1523656980

Other business and technology books by Jeff Jochum

- Foxpro 2.1 — A Developer's Guide (coauthor, M&T Books 1991)
- Fast Tack to Clipper (M&T Books 1993)
- E-business for E-bozos (EBZ.com 1997)
- Unreasonable Thoughts (Unleashing Your Creativity) (Team-X.biz Press 2012)
- Work Happily Ever-After (Photographer Edition) (Team-X.biz Press 2013)

Contents

PREFACE...1
ARE YOU IN THE RIGHT PLACE? 5
  Who Is This Book For?.. 5
  Who Is This Book Not For? 6
  Brand Identity, Value, and Declaration 7

INTRODUCTION 9
  Brand Loyalty Isn't Dead.................................. 10
  Loyalty and Trust Have Become Synonyms.......... 14
  Why Buy You?... 15
IN THE BEGINNING..19
  Jack of All Trades? 19
  The Marketing Law of Division........................21
  Specialism Marches On..................................22
DEMOGRAPHICS: THE BIG LIE 25
  The Double Xs 28
  They Are You..30
TRUST LEADERSHIP..31

THE LAW OF BRAND SPECIALISM.................... 35
WHAT IS SPECIALISM? 37
  Generalist versus Specialist............................37
  What (Exactly) Is an Authentically Unique Brand?....38
  Specialty or Commodity.................................. 40

SECTION 1: BRAND IDENTITY........................ 43
ELEMENT 101: UNIQUENESS 45
  What's in Your Soup?......................................46
  Authenticity Words 48
ELEMENT 102: SIMPLICITY 51
  Complexification 53
  A Need to Know..55
  Authenticity Hates Complexity........................56
ELEMENT 103: STICKINESS.................................59
  Selling Food to Hungry People.........................60
  Stories Are Sticky 61
  The Information Paradox.................................64
ELEMENT 104: BETTER.......................................67

Different from Better 69
The World's Best Entrepreneurs 69
ELEMENT 105: QUALITY 73
"It Works!" 74
Something We Can Lose and Never Gain 75
A TRANSFORMATION STORY: JENNIFER CHANEY 77

SECTION 2: BRAND VALUE 81
ELEMENT 201: COMPETITION 83
The Test of Opposites 85
Winning without Competing 86
ELEMENT 202: POLARIZATION 89
Demonizing Your Competition 90
Love Your Enemies 92
ELEMENT 203: IMPERFECTION 95
Guilty Pleasures Will Set You Free 98
ELEMENT 204: SIGNATURES 101
Naming Your Rose 102
ELEMENT 205: PERFORMANCE 105
Performance versus Product Business Models 106
A TRANSFORMATION STORY: SHOOTDOTEDIT.COM 109

SECTION 3: BRAND EXECUTION 113
ELEMENT 301: CHOICES 115
Customers Lie 117
Why People Buy 118
The Power of Focus 119
Changing Is Harder 120
ELEMENT 302: INFLUENCE 121
Personal Trumps Social 122
ELEMENT 303: DISCOUNTING 125
The Groupon Failure 126
ELEMENT 304: PROGRESS 129
Flying versus Not Falling 130
Activity versus Progress 132
ELEMENT 305: SELLING 133
Selling to an Unsophisticated Client 135
A TRANSFORMATION STORY: ME RA KOH 137

NEXT STEPS..**143**

THE CULT OF YOU..145

    Creating Your Own Love Potion.......................................*146*

    The Real Secret Ingredient..*147*

    Some Final Cautions..*149*

    On-Demand Education..*150*

    Online Communities..*150*

    Work with Me...*151*

ACKNOWLEDGMENTS...153

ABOUT THE AUTHOR...159

BIBLIOGRAPHY 161

To Mom and Dad, who always knew what I was capable of (best and worst) and never lost faith in the best. To my kids, who ignore my worst and only see my best. And to my wife, Mary Ellen, who relentlessly helps me discover a better best.

Preface

As you may have discovered from the description of this book, many of the ideas contained in *Uniqueing Your Brand* were entrusted to me decades ago by very smart people. They did so because other very smart people had previously trusted them with these principles and they found success using them in their businesses, as I have. For over thirty years, I've studied, evolved, and safeguarded this secret science. Now, it's my time to share it with newer, smarter minds.

When I was initially gifted this knowledge, there were no specific requirements placed on me to share with others or keep them to myself, or even any implied ethical use. Like other sciences, the chemistry of *specialism* (my term for this knowledge) is complete in its objectivity and proven effectiveness, leaving the ultimate aim of its results—altruistic or otherwise—entirely to the scientist.

By releasing these secrets, I am confident many of you will cultivate and evolve it. However, I am not as objective about this as my predecessors and hope (and expect) those of you enabled by this knowledge will use these *elements of specialism* (revealed here, for the first time) to make the business world a place that increasingly values *authenticity*, rather than one that gets better at faking it. It's in your hands, now.

Be ethical. Be empathetic. Be wise.

It has been said that we can see as far as we do only because we stand on the shoulders of those who came before us. This book is a testament to that.

As a result, you will see many quotes from those whom I encountered while researching this book.

I ask you to take note of these referenced authors (in the bibliography) and seek out their teachings. My summaries, arguments, and quotes are not a sufficient substitute for actually reading, learning, and reaching your own conclusions about what they said firsthand.

As I said, prior to the three years I spent crafting this book, I spent *thirty* years evaluating, learning, testing, teaching, thought-experimenting, learning some more, overcoming countless dead ends, and finally *applying* this revolutionary chemistry to my own business endeavors, to repeated successes.

All of the elements defined here have been proven effective in all types of business models and marketing strategies. Once you *activate* them by adding your authentically unique content, the results you want will begin to materialize. The sooner you start testing your own "formulas" in the marketplace, the faster you'll achieve your unique success.

On a related note, let me offer another important lesson I have learned about succeeding, and in turn teach my own teams, businesses clients, and students:

You don't learn anything important from success (since it mostly reinforces what you already knew or suspected.)

I have discovered that "failures" are the most productive sources of entrepreneurial education.

And to get the most from those experiences, I urge you to avoid the "reasonable" response when dealing with them; e.g. covering them up, sweeping them under the rug, or denying their existence altogether.

Instead, I challenge you to take the UNreasonable approach and *embrace failures* so you may gain the valuable benefits of a very difficult experience. For what it's worth, being unreasonable has been one of my greatest success tools. I learned it from this guy.

> *The reasonable man adapts him[her]self to the world; the unreasonable one persists in trying to adapt the world to him[her]self. Therefore, all progress depends on the unreasonable man [or woman].*
>
> *– George Bernard Shaw* (1903)

Finally, note that I wanted this book to be "short" while still delivering the full story of specialism as well as being useful as a reference book, where you can return easily to re-experience and reinforce the lessons contained in each Elemental chapter. With that goal, I have worked hard to distill my elephantine first draft into the concentrated 170 pages before you. I hope that makes it easier to learn.

Completing the metaphor, *Uniqueing Your Brand* is meant to be experienced like a well-aged, highly potent brandy instead of a boxed wine. While they're both made from grapes, they otherwise have very little in common.

So grab a snifter and let's go.

Are You in the Right Place?

This book is written for small-business owners, professional-service providers, and entrepreneurs who are not as fulfilled or profitable as they'd like to be in their efforts. By clearly defining your authentic uniqueness and declaring it to the world, you can reach higher peaks of success than you ever thought possible.

Over the last thirty years, the concepts defined here in *Uniqueing Your Brand* have worked for passionate, self-reliant, creative entrepreneurs at all levels of growth. Whether you don't yet have a business and want to know the best way to get started, you're burned out after many years of seeing where you want to be but are unable to quite get there, or you're anywhere in between, the answers are in this book.

Who Is This Book For?

- **Committed, Ambitious, and Impatient Beginners.** Want to launch a new creative business or re-launch into a new category or market? *Uniqueing Your Brand* will keep you focused on the right goals and achievements while avoiding the fatal and unproductive chasms.

- **Frustrated Creative Entrepreneurs.** Many (*many*) of my most successful graduates arrived on my doorstep ready to give it all up. Sure, they're respected and successful and, in some cases, famous—but something important was missing.

- **Anyone Who Feels Trapped in the *Groundhog Day* Movie.** Do you feel forced to do what you *used* to love, every day? Has it become just another reminder that "it" isn't there anymore?

- **Teachers, Coaches, and Anyone Who Has Heard the Call to Help Others.** You are a creative professional, author, personal-service entrepreneur, business coach, brand consultant, or subject-matter expert who wants to develop a truly unique brand presence, build your platform and fan base fast, earn a great living from it all, *and* help others find the key to working happily.

Who Is This Book *Not* For?

- ❖ **Werewolf Hunters.** Those who believe there is a silver bullet to success. I'm honored to have thousands of successful program graduates from around the world, and every one of them has worked *hard* to achieve their happy success. *Building* your success and happiness is our mutual goal and at the core of what this book and I are all about. If you don't succeed (and exceed), then I don't either.

- ❖ **Chameleons.** Those who are willing to "become what they need to be" to succeed. I believe that you cannot achieve *sustainable* success by sacrificing your authenticity at the altar of convenience. This book *can* help you find *yourself* inside your business, guide you in describing your purpose with clarity, and show you how to work happily ever after.

- ❖ **Logo Addicts.** No one ever got—or lost—the job because of a fancy logo, cool business card, or snappy tagline, and I have no interest in wasting your time pursuing them. By focusing on a unique, genuine, and clear business purpose, you will discover how quickly these other things become unimportant.

❖ **Bargainers.** Those who seek the best deal over the best experience. See "Demographics: The Big Lie" for a full explanation of this.

❖ **Get-Rich-Quickers.** No educational program works unless you do. If you're expecting this book—or anything else—to magically solve your problems or make you money, please put it down and get a full refund. *Uniqueing Your Brand* is not some get-rich-quick scheme. I actually care that you implement the ideas in this book. I have learned that if you focus on creating and delivering an authentic brand, you can achieve results in your business and your life that you likely thought impossible. I'm challenging you to think differently, to behave differently, and to become the businessperson you're meant to be.

Brand Identity, Value, and Declaration

After a brief introduction and history, we'll jump straight into the foundational **Law of Brand Specialism**, followed by the Elements that are the fundamental chemistry of *Uniqueing Your Brand*.

I have divided this information into three sections:

1. Brand Identity (Discovery)

2. Brand Value (Definition)

3. Brand Execution (Declaration)

In **Section 1 – Brand Identity**, you'll *discover* how *you* are at the core of your brand and how embracing your authentically real self will dramatically change the success trajectory of your business.

Section 2 – Brand Value will show you how adopting an authentically unique brand as a core business ideal positively affects your life, team, clients, and prospects and why they will be compelled to want you.

Section 3 – Brand Execution will empower you to *deliver* your authentic and unique value to the marketplace by enhancing your message through increased focus and proven marketing techniques. It will help you to make tough choices, understand the upside of not being loved by everyone, and drive your own success forward.

Finally, in the **Next Steps** section, I'll give you some parting advice on what to look out for and a link to some of my online lessons and resources so that your journey to AUB success doesn't have to end here.

Also, note that at the end of each section are *real-world* examples of personal businesses that have embraced and succeeded with their authentically unique declarations. I call these **Transformation Stories**, and they will give you insights into how and why the science of specialism actually changes lives.

Introduction

The report of my death is an exaggeration.

— *Mark Twain* (1897)

This book is about magic.

And science.

And business.

And blending them together, which I think of as

Alchemy.

Alchemy is defined at Dictionary.com as "any magical power or process of transmuting a common substance into a substance of great value." The best-known example of that transformation of a *common substance into a substance of great value* is the legend that alchemists could turn lead into gold.

To be clear, I certainly can't make any promises that what you learn in this book will cause some mysterious transformation of metals.

What I can promise is that we'll be creating serious marketing magic during the course of this book. Especially, if you see your *current* brand message as the *common substance* and an authentically unique brand as the *substance of great value*.

OK, so if this book is about magic and science and you and your business, what kind of "magic" will you learn here?

- The magic of easily creating true brand loyalty.

- The magic of effortlessly increasing "good" profits.

- The magic of attracting customers you love and love you back.

All of that magic will be explained using the clarity of science and the elements of a psychological chemistry that makes it all happen. By the time you get done with *Uniqueing Your Brand*, you will be able to turn a market of anonymous prospects into a loyal community of high-value customers, just like those of us before you.

In the world of business, that's as close to turning lead into gold as anyone ever gets.

Brand Loyalty Isn't Dead.

While it must be clear by now that this book is rooted in the science of specialism, in execution it is focused squarely on loyalty.

Brand loyalty.

"How can that be?" you may be asking, "I thought brand loyalty *was* dead." You aren't alone in thinking this. In his book *The Loyalty Effect*, Frederick Reichheld also ponders whether loyalty is dead.

On average, U.S. corporations now lose half their customers in five years, half their employees in four, and half their investors in less than one, we seem to face a future in which the only business relationships will be opportunistic transaction between strangers. (Reichheld and Teal, 1996)

He goes on to make a strong argument that loyalty not only still lives, but also *remains* a powerhouse of value to those companies that understand how to identify, measure, and leverage it. Since Mr. Reichheld is considered by most as the preeminent expert on loyalty, I'd have thought that the question of whether loyalty still exists had been put to rest. Not so much.

In researching this book, I've spoken to a lot of other experts and found many predicting—or bemoaning—the ongoing demise of customer loyalty to branded products and services. This included lots of hand wringing, head shaking, and what-are-we-going-to-do-now looks.

Like Mark Twain's erroneously reported death over one hundred years ago (quoted at the top of this chapter,) the reports of brand loyalty's death have also been highly exaggerated. I have defined three groups of "mourners" who ironically all agree on the source of its impending demise—the tsunami of information that is the Internet—yet differ on the actual *reason why* they believe it will ultimately expire.

The first group of hand wringers is the simplest to understand in their cause-and-effect logic. This group believes that the Internet's information wave is simply overwhelming people with too many choices, triggering our natural bias toward *analysis paralysis*—a state in which the consumer experiences an inability to effectively compare options and, as a result, feels dissatisfied with *any* choice. Their logic concludes that if consumers can't be satisfied with their decisions on anything, then they won't develop a loyalty to anything, as well.

On its face this makes some sense—until you realize that people are psychologically wired for loyalty even more strongly than they are wired for indecision. As a member of a *tribe*, we yearn for the connection that loyalty affords us, and this is stronger than the fear of making a bad choice. The fact that eight billion people haven't isolated themselves away behind eight billion locked doors just to feel "safe" is proof enough of this.

The second group of mourners is more nuanced. That perspective is expressed accurately by Itamar Simonson and Emanuel Rosen, authors of the book *Absolute Value*, who start out well, arguing that the concept of information *overload* is largely a myth.

> *These days you hear so much about information overload and its paralyzing effects on decision making that sometimes you wonder how consumers make decisions at all. While we agree that people face unprecedented amounts of information (and that indeed some are overwhelmed by it), most consumers can handle the information just fine.* (2004)

They make an interesting additional point stating that the historical rise of brands was in response to information *poor*, rather than information overloaded, environments. Since the web is delivering the full, deep data that people want, they conclude, consumers *no longer have a need to develop any brand loyalty, since every choice is built on a new set of inputs.*

For me, that premise falters in the implied conclusion that consumers have learned to *start fresh* with every decision because they know how quickly products change. Does this constant feature creep really remove the need for a repeated brand experience—a fundamental pillar of loyalty? If so, it would certainly be a big step in proving that brand loyalty is becoming obsolete.

However, this conclusion seems paradoxical and counter-intuitive, and the social sciences are clear that it is unproven and unrealistic to assume that people both consume an abundance of information while still "starting fresh" with every decision. Every human I've ever known—including me—is far too efficient (i.e. lazy) for that much decision-making effort to occur.

In fact, this conclusion also conflicts with the basic psychological bias of *framing*, wherein we struggle with the importance of what we already know when attempting to learn new skills. It is a common educational belief that the biggest hurdle to learning something new is *experience*.

Finally, there is the group that believes the more we know, the less we believe. They lay the blame for this on a growing skepticism that is the by-product of a well-informed audience constantly feeding on the web's "unlimited" information stream.

This view can be best illustrated by W. C. Field's quote: "You can't cheat an honest man; never give a sucker an even break, or smarten up a chump" (1939). It also seems totally relevant in reflecting Simonson and Rosen's view of the current market's overall distrust.

And who can blame the more cautious among us, with the constant flow of lurid stories of dirty dealings, dishonest politicians, and greedy CEOs usually making the biggest news headlines? It may seem that being an "honest man" has become the worst thing to be, since any kind of loyalty — brand or otherwise — is something only "suckers" would have.

I think all of these conclusions are inaccurate, and will spend the bulk of this book showing you how and why brand loyalty is growing faster than ever. Simply, I believe the problem is one of perception. Brand loyalty isn't dying; it has simply become harder to *see* since it is more selective and not as universal as it once was.

Brand loyalty is no longer tied to the features, benefits, or taglines of products or services; instead, it is becoming increasingly attached to something much more special and harder to deliver.

Trust.

The *new* brand loyalty is tied to trust: the trust a company creates in the minds of its marketplace with its brand message; the trust in a company's motives; the trust in what a team "stands for" at its essence; the trust in the relationships it creates with its customers; and, ultimately, **the trust in a brand's authentic purpose**.

That kind of trust is only created when the customer understands *why* a company does what it does and exactly *who* it is trying to benefit. The kind of trust created by an *authentically unique brand*.

Loyalty and Trust Have Become Synonyms.

Historically, while brand loyalty started as a dependency on how things were *made*, it now lives at the center of a company's *purpose*. And since the creation of each company's purpose is so personal, intimate, and human, the resulting brand message must embody that unique, authentic humanness within it or be called out as false, contrived, or mercenary.

As consumers, we've become innately aware of the genuine one-of-a-kindness that now lives at the core of the new brand loyalty. This is why I am convinced loyalty to authentically unique brands is stronger than ever and just getting more valuable as all other types of product-centric loyalty diminishes.

Sure, we still expect, and depend on, a certain level of quality in all the products we consume; we just no longer confuse dependable with trusted.

Over the next many chapters, I'll show you how to bake that new brand loyalty directly into your message without forcing you to make any core changes to your business goals or purpose.

In fact, this process really creates **more**: *more* of what your best customers already love, *more* of what your business does best, and results in *more* customers on your doorstep.

And it all begins with…

Why Buy You?

Why *should* your customers buy from *you* instead of your competitors?

If you think an answer to this question is based in any way on the superior quality of your product, then please take one step back, shake your head vigorously, and uncap your mind. You're in for a shock.

In his book *TILT*, Niraj Dawar does a wonderful job of putting this *quality-first* mind-set into perspective.

Products are important, of course. For decades, businesses sought competitive advantage almost exclusively in activities related to new product creation.

[Note: By *product creation* he means building bigger factories, sourcing cheaper raw materials or labor and more efficient ways to transport and fulfill, and inventing products that competitors presumably could not easily replicate.]

But these sources of competitive advantages are being irreversibly leveled by globalization and technology. Today, competitors can rapidly decipher and deploy the recipe for your product's secret sauce and use it against you. (2013)

Let me simplify that a bit more. *The competitive advantage that comes from how products are **made** – a.k.a. quality – has disappeared.* This doesn't mean that competitive advantage is a thing of the past. Rather, its baseline has shifted, and it is now found more in the product or service *experience,* where companies interact more intimately with customers in the marketplace.

This means that the *experience* you or your company creates is now more important to your *brand promise* than a feature or benefit of any product you produce or sell.

It also means that what makes you *authentically unique* is now your most powerful secret sauce and the key source of brand loyalty. It is something no one can copy or take away from you or your business. (Which is also the First Law of Specialism.) Attaining this level of brand authenticity is the primary goal of specialism and *Uniqueing Your Brand.*

To be clear, a business **brand** must describe how a customer *feels* about your business and exists solely to attract other customers who can benefit from your company's products or services. It creates a visual, emotional, and cultural connection between customers and your company, conjuring up powerful images for them, consciously and subconsciously.

A successful brand unambiguously declares your purpose while crystallizing the value of your product or service to customers in their expectations.

Brands come in two primary flavors. The first is *brand differentiation* and focuses on how to define yourself or your company as distinctive compared to others in the market. By emphasizing your comparative advantage as part of your brand identity, you can position your products or services to stand out in the market and, presumably, attract more customers.

A differentiation brand advantage can range anywhere from innovative product design to having the lowest price in your market.

The second flavor — and the overall concentration of this book — is *brand uniqueness*, where the focus is based on one-of-a-kindness, rather than comparison. This is a way for you to declare why you are **special** and how that enhances your product or service without making it only a comparative reflection of your competition.

Here, your value is directly connected to what your brand *stands for* and how that will also enhance your customers' lives or experiences. As implied already, I have officially termed this an **Authentically Unique Brand** (AUB); its advantage is often tied to your purpose or mission and reflects the authentic values driving your company and customers.

Note that a differentiation brand is easier to launch and harder to sustain because it is increasingly dependent on market comparisons, and whenever a competitor improves or changes, your differentiation-based identity must adjust as well.

In contrast, an Authentically Unique Brand based on your one-of-a-kindness is tougher to define and launch — since it has to be both self-contained and authentic — and is much easier to maintain over a long term because it's a reflection of what you naturally believe in, and doesn't change based on market characteristics.

In all cases, when customers buy your brand, they're buying *you*.

Your values.

Your promises.

Your purpose.

For your brand to be successful, it must help customers to feel that their own values and expectations are aligned with yours. You, the customers, and the product or service you deliver must enhance the relationship between you and them for your brand message to have any hope of creating a true loyalty.

In the Beginning...

All business *categories* begin life as orphans.

Cameras, computers, cars—and their human counterparts: photographers, programmers, and drivers—all start out as generalized deliverables, designed to address the broadest scope of both known and unknown uses. Over time, the resulting products and services become more clearly defined by dividing and subdividing to create a multitude of subcategories, each with a narrower and more specialized approach than the original category.

Jack of All Trades?

Stepping back, let's lay some groundwork for this discussion of brand *value*. Business growth isn't as complex as most business books would have you believe. In fact, like most things, it becomes easier to grasp when you simplify it into broader categories. For example, I believe there are only three phases of entrepreneurial business growth.

The first is the *designer* ("engineering") phase, in which you have created something—product, service, technology—that you believe people will want to pay for, so you search for real customers to prove it. Key concepts here are *innovation* and *disruption*.

The second phase is the *generalist* ("sales"). Here, you've proven that your product or service has some demand, yet that demand may be less specific than you originally thought. As a result, you will modify your product or service—and your price—as needed to sell to anyone who has the money to pay for it, even if it isn't in line with your original goals and expectations. Key concepts here are *flexible* and *revenue driven*.

Finally, once you achieve enough sales stability to reach the *specialism* ("marketing") phase, you become free to clearly define how the product or service *should* be used—and at what price—focusing all your resources on refining it to that specific result and selling only to customers who want exactly that. Specialism is relentless in its demand to narrow your target, even when it means shattering the original general category that birthed it. Key concepts here are *focused* and *profitable*.

Ultimately, only deep-pocket businesses can survive for very long in the designer phase, and many failures also occur when businesses try to remain in the generalist phase for too long, frightened by the obvious risk and effort needed to evolve into specialism.

Here's the rub: if you are in a business that *can be* disrupted by the Internet, choosing the "do everything" approach for very long is *generally* a costly mistake. (Pun intended.)

As the World Wide Web becomes ubiquitous in a particular business sector, the generalist's days are numbered. I've seen the web devour endless volumes of businesses since I began tracking this behavior in 1990—about the same time the Internet started exploding.

With consumers having increased access to specialized products and services directly from expert sources, this evolution now happens to all industries. Adding to the problem is that most widely accepted small-business marketing strategies, like *quality first, work longer hours,* and *demographic targeting,* are outdated and ineffective.

The Marketing Law of Division

In 1993, Al Ries and Jack Trout published one of the great business books of the twentieth century titled *The 22 Immutable Laws of Marketing*. To lay the foundation for an AUB, understanding their Law of Division is very important.

They defined it this way: "Over time, a category will divide and become two or more categories" (2009). This law warns us that we can anticipate that customer choice demands will always increase as a category evolves. This Law of Division lives at the heart of a unique branding. Although a simple concept, it can get very complicated in execution and rarely happens quickly.

For an Authentically Unique Brand to succeed, it must be more than slogans and snappy taglines.

It must represent a personal authenticity and declare why being *you* is a very important part of what you do or the product or company you represent. In a word, an AUB requires you, and your business, to have *clarity* of purpose. Without that, your brand will ring hollow, and so will the experiences of you, your team, and your customers.

As mentioned, industries don't simply divide and subdivide randomly. Rather, division occurs when expertise drives the market to greater efficiency and the solution is a narrowed focus on very specific areas of the category.

Using photography as an example, that market didn't divide itself based on black-and-white images versus color images. It segmented based on very specific and evolved philosophies and practices that occurred within the general category of photography, like film versus digital.

In fact, we see entirely new cameras being created to enable photographers at all levels to focus on *increasingly* narrow types of photography, whether it's video, stills, 360 degree image capture, or something brand new that will come out next quarter.

While I discuss this in more detail in the "Better" chapter, for now I submit that entrepreneurs can actually meet and exceed the expectations of their clients who are otherwise overwhelmed with an endless array of choices. The AUB clearly defines the question for them while at the same time supplying an expert and personalized answer.

Specialism Marches On

To further illustrate, witness how the original pinhole camera ultimately spawned a plethora of more advanced and specialized devices: SLRs, DSLRs, point-and-shoots, video cameras, and the ever-present phone cameras.

Similarly, the "big iron" room-sized computers were replaced by mini, micro, desktop, laptop, and tablet computers, and the hand-built Daimler automobiles grew (and shrank) into everything from the Model T to Mack Trucks to Formula-1 race cars to Teslas.

Understandably, the service of these product categories also moved from the general to the specialized as the skills needed to maximize the products' capabilities into more discrete use cases became critical.

Again, nowhere is this more obvious than with cameras, where generalist photographers have been *forced* to evolve into increasingly refined specializations like weddings, high-school seniors, families, portraits, boudoir, births, and even education of parents on how to use phone cameras to take photos of their kids.

These are all examples of steps toward Authentically Unique Brands, and were *initially* powerful enough to elevate the brand message above the generalist masses.

Twenty years ago, if you used the word *only* in your pitch, (e.g., "I *only* repair Mercedes") you'd have been on the cutting edge of specialization.

Now, these simple *I-only-do-that* declarations are no longer truly considered specializations at all. They've evolved into less special niches rather than specialized focus areas, i.e. it is something everyone has learned to declare in order to *appear* special. The problem, of course, is that when everyone is declaring a similar specialness, the marketplace will see no one as truly special.

In today's market, for your brand to be seen as specialized, it must hone your message to a sharp point of uniqueness. And there's no better way to do that than to center on what makes you genuinely special as a *person*. The stuff that makes you *you!*

Why does this matter? Well... who are your ideal prospective clients? Note that, in most cases, they are a lot like *you*. By that I don't necessarily mean they are like you in age, income, location, marital status, or some other demographic. In truth, those similarities have little effect when considering the power of an Authentically Unique Brand. (We'll explore this more in the next chapter.)

Rather, they are like you in how they *behave*. How do they view their place in the world? What makes them part with their money in exchange for someone else's (your!) time or products? So, how do they choose? We'll explore the chasm between demographics and behavior in great detail in the next chapter.

Demographics: The Big Lie

QUESTION: What do the Easter Bunny, an honest politician, and the high-end consumer all have in common?

ANSWER: None of them really exists.

While the Easter Bunny and the honest politician may come as no surprise, why is *high-end consumer* in that list? If they don't really exist, why are there hundreds (or even thousands) of books, classes, workshops, and entire industries predicated on enticing you with how to find, attract, pitch, and sell to this elusive customer profile?

First, let's deflate the idea of high-end or even upscale consumers, since it is based on the inaccurate assumption that we can predict the behavior of people by categorizing their age, education, location, income level, and other general bits of information. These points of data are referred to as *demographics*, and they have driven much marketing theory, and execution for a century or more. Here's the thing:

For entrepreneurial, creative, and service-based businesses, demographics aren't as predictive as many experts would have you believe. Honestly, they never were.

Wait. If they're not effective, why are they still considered the "safe" way of marketing? That answer may surprise you, as well.

When we don't have any real informative data that helps us understand the *behavior* of the market, we use what information we have. This is often the easily obtained demographic data that is available everywhere, in volumes. We choose it, even when we *know* it is largely ineffective for our purpose. Why? Because we think is all we have to work with.

I call that compromise "The Big Lie."

Nobody has ever been entirely successful using demographics as the key behavioral indicator. Instead, they are often forced to compromise and depend on social data (e.g., stories, examples, and anecdotes) that only reinforce foregone analytical conclusions.

This is why I focused on the marketing ideology of *behavioral specialism* in the first place. My goal of depending strictly on social and behavioral research (known as *psychographics*) comes from the commonsense requirement to add behavior to our analysis — simply put, how people *act* rather than simply who they *are*.

The reason that this type of analysis is so much harder than using demographics is because the behavioral data must be studied over long periods of time across geographically and culturally diverse groups of people to be valid. This takes a lot of patience and resources — certainly more than most marketing departments can allocate.

By comparison, demographics are much simpler to compile since they're usually based on existing poll data about geography, ethnicity, education, income, and so forth. Hence, marketers tend to believe more strongly in demographics than social and behavioral-science analysis, even though they know that demographics aren't very accurate for predicting the behavior of a market. This is partly because demographics are more readily available and partly because of the *anchoring bias*, which psychology tells us is the belief that the stuff we already know is more valuable than the stuff we don't know, yet. Additionally, behavioral-science data is simply more scarce and harder to get. Sure, that's not a rational conclusion, but...

Human minds are staggeringly irrational.

Luckily, psychographic research has grown in popularity, sophistication and efficiency over the last few decades, and the results have given us an insight into *why* consumers act a certain way under certain circumstances — regardless of how irrational that behavior may seem — with increasing scientific accuracy. There are many studies and books dedicated to this emerging view of "predictably irrational," with the best being written by Dan Ariely.

More to my point, the value of psychographic data was recently highlighted in a very broad study conducted by Roy Morgan Research, one of the world's oldest and largest consumer-research firms, at the request of authors Ross Honeywill and Christopher Norton for their book *113 Million Markets of One*. They report:

> *Accessing hundreds of thousands of survey respondents, we were able to put together more than two billion points of data, from an impeccable, independent, single source, Roy Morgan Research, collecting information on three continents, including the U.S.A.* (2012)

At the core of their research was ten years of data spread over a million consumers and their findings demonstrate the power of accurate and specific social and behavioral analysis.

For me, reading and researching this information was a personal turning point in that it scientifically proved many of the conclusions I had already discovered from using these secret elements about why and how people buy. Finally, with real data rather than just anecdotal experience (and the elemental secrets granted me, of course) to back up my observations about the nature of Brand Specialism, I was able to divine how to identify and attract very different consumer behaviors. And now I'll show you.

The Double Xs

Back to the high-end consumer. Why am I saying that he or she simply doesn't exist? As I've stated, the concept of an upscale anything is rooted in demographics, and isn't dependably accurate. Just because consumers *have* money to spend doesn't mean they are actually *open* to spending it. And it certainly doesn't mean that they'll want to spend it on you. This brings us to two fundamental questions:

- *How can we know what people will spend their money on?*

- *How can we use that information to make your business more successful?*

OK, so we now know that customers fit into behavioral categories. On the conservative side, there are *bargainers* who buy based on status (brand-name safety), features, and price. Collectively, these factors are called *the deal*. The bargainer's goal is to seek out "the deal too good to pass up," and that is often the only way to get them to spend their money.

According to Ray Morgan Research, bargainers represent *"52 percent of adults, who amazingly accounted for only 23 percent of discretionary spending. When it came to spending, they were attracted to a combination of status, features, price, and deals"* — that is, your products and services — and only 4 percent of them are considered "big spenders" in their self-described behavior (Honeywill and Norton, 2012).

Going after bargainers means you have to ensure that every deal you make with them is *too good to pass up.* That generally means pricing below your competitors — a race to the bottom — resulting in profit margins too low to support growth and success. From an Authentically Unique Branded company perspective, price discounting is like selling off your family, one kid at a time, at fire-sale prices.

On the other side of that consumer coin, we have the *explorers* and *exclusives* — collectively, I call them *Double Xs* — who spend money on things that reflect their distinctive values, which are primarily based on authenticity, discovery, individuality, and exclusivity.

Double Xs represent 48 percent of the population, while being responsible for 77 percent of discretionary spending! Better yet, a whopping 92 percent of them describe themselves as "big spenders."

The best news of all is that they absolutely dominate every age category under fifty. The Double Xs are the emerging market category, and Honeywell and Norton believe that within ten years, they will dominate every area of business (2012).

For Authentically Unique Brand businesses, Double Xs are your primary target — not the demographically high-end of anything. This is why trying to find, chase, and sell to bargainers is a waste of your time, money, and resources. If you are doing this now, **stop it.**

You're welcome.

They Are You

How do you find and attract the Double X consumers to your business? First, it helps to know that *they* are a lot like *you*. I have discovered that *entrepreneurs* are four times as likely to be Double Xs as bargainers

Further, "They are not attracted to conspicuous consumption (status brands) and have a highly individualized view of the world, looking to express their own values through what they buy, what they do, and who they do it with." (Honeywill and Norton, 2012).

Sound familiar?

There are some really strong brand identities out there focusing *very* successfully on Double Xs, including Lululemon, Mini Cooper, Anthropologie, and, of course, Apple. If you consider these brands representative of you, then you are likely a Double X consumer.

Knowing that Double Xs are looking for authentic businesses that reinforce what they stand for, the easy answer to attracting them is to do the same. Build a business that is authentic and passionate and that connects with them on a very personal level. Becoming a *trust leader* is critical if you wish to be one of tomorrow's successful entrepreneurs.

Trust Leadership

Every marketing book, workshop, and seminar I've encountered over the last few decades all have something in common: they advise finding and focusing on "thought leaders" in whatever industry or niche you are trying to gain success with. Thought leaders are further identified as the influencers you need to get on your side if you expect your marketing message to catch on.

Until the day the Internet became ubiquitous, this was great advice. However, the concept of influence has now taken on a different profile in that increased (and totally legitimate) skepticism presumes that all spokespeople have an agenda—a personal interest in whatever they happen to be recommending. As a result, influence is no longer tied solely to being *known*. (This is explored in more detail in the "Influence" chapter.)

What is still true is that people desire and need influencers who guide them to decisions and information they would otherwise find too difficult or time-consuming to make or locate for themselves. They still need a trusted opinion.

Enter the replacement for the thought leader: the *trust* leader.

Where thought leaders used expertise and objectivity, trust leaders use personal experience and admitted self-interest. They don't value expertise as much as community and authenticity. They're focused on gaining your trust and loyalty by being transparent about their purpose and perspective, and they that understand trust is earned, not bought or cajoled—especially when it comes to brand loyalty.

They know brand trust is the result of creating value for the community that they are part of. They see team members and partners as trust *assets*, not simply points of revenue opportunities or channels for marketing promotions.

As businesses, trust leaders often create or nurture *mutual* companies, where the needs of the company and its customers are demonstrably more important than those of people outside their company (e.g., shareholders, Wall Street, competitors, detractors) because they are actually owned (either physically or ideologically) by their community.

A great example of this is **State Farm Insurance**, a mutual company that is owned entirely by its policyholders. Any profits earned by a mutual insurance company are rebated to policyholders in the form of dividend distributions or reduced future premiums. State Farm is a trust leader both in their industry and in their corporate community.

Even if your company isn't a mutual company by the letter of that definition, you can still gain great value in the market by following that guidance to stand out as a trust leader.

Allow yourself to be led by your mutual (i.e. shared-purpose) community.

In addition to understanding how brand trust is created, trust leaders also know that retention is more important than immediate revenue and are happy to advertise that fact to their community whenever they can.

Too often I've seen business leaders torch their brand trust at the altar of new-customer acquisition. By constantly focusing their marketing efforts on ways to reward people for joining the community, they fail to see that the existing community is feeling increasingly isolated and taken for granted.

Loyalty, like charity, begins at home.

Even events like customer summits or conferences, which are specifically meant to elevate and reward customer longevity and loyalty, often get hijacked by sales and become one big opportunity to attract and close new customers. ("Bring a friend and it's free to you" messages are the worst for this.) Nobody feels rewarded when they know their key value to the community is as leverage to gain access to their friends as sales prospects.

Additionally, trust leaders know that market share, cost position, and service quality no longer guarantee success. A quick review of the histories of old-school businesses like car manufacturers reinforces this. There is no longer any hill so high that someone else will not be able to climb it to kick you off.

You know who knows this very well? Google (now Alphabet.) They are pulling out all of the stops to create very specialized communities for each of their products and/or services, without losing their purpose of "gathering all the world's information into one place."

You know who doesn't seem to understand it, at the time of this writing? Apple; who is increasing aloof to the value of their own, amazing community. This change in community focus may ultimately be the beginning of the end for their market supremacy... or they may still (hopefully) wake up.

Author's note: It will be interesting to watch over the next decade whether Apple is able to overcome its comfortably dominant position and compete with Google/Alphabet, who doesn't seem to take anything for granted.

Finally, trust leaders seem to inherently understand the differences between productive profits and destructive money. Not all profits are created equal, and not all costs are the same to attain new customers.

Interestingly, this is where both Apple and Google excel — in ensuring that their marketing chemistry is targeting those consumers who *want* to spend their money with them. Their customers gain a deeper satisfaction than simply an exchange of values. In the best cases, an AUB makes it *self-actualizing* (more on this in the next chapter) to buy from a company you are emotionally connected to.

The Uniqueing Your Brand *profit formula* is simple: an AUB draws the best customers to your company or service by creating brand loyalty and trust. This then attracts the best employees and partners and results in long-term relationships that reduce costs and increase value, thereby increasing productivity and creating a cost advantage that rewards everyone in that circle of trust.

So without trust, there is no loyalty. And all brand loyalty requires the voice of a trust leader (that's you). So let's get started on making you the best of the best. Step one is using the foundation on which all of this brand trust is built: Specialism.

The Law of Brand Specialism

Anyone can copy what you do.
No one can copy who you are.

What would you say if I asked you, "What makes you special in the eyes of your client?"

Over the last few decades of working alongside and coaching creative entrepreneurs, I often start with that exact question. These are the most common responses:

- "I'm passionate."
- "I'm a professional."
- "I'm authentic."

Although these things may seem valuable, direct, and special; they are really only better than bad. This becomes most obvious when we review the opposite meanings or antonyms for each word. For example, by saying that you are passionate, professional, and real, you are really only defining yourself as *better* than someone who claims to be the opposite: bored, amateurish, and fake.

Of course, no business will ever express claims like that, which means you are elevating yourself above a competitor (whether real or perceived) that simply can't exist; making you more special than *no one*.

A quick historical review demonstrates that when an industry sector or market evolves to the point of sparking specialists, it quickly turns into a wildfire. This happens in part because successful specialists no longer feel the need to hide the secret of their success from others, for fear of being copied or plagiarized.

Their marketing "sauce" is no longer something that can be diminished or taken, so they no longer feel afraid of competition. There is always a high demand for true specialists, regardless of how many there are. In fact, the more you cultivate your AUB, the less true competition ultimately exists.

What is Specialism?

Specialism is at the heart of Authentically Unique Brands and can be broadly defined as the *philosophical devotion to a unique pursuit*.

Most dictionaries also define it as a synonym for *specialty* or *specialization*. I think that isn't 100 percent accurate. The suffix *-ism* is defined as a "distinctive doctrine, theory, or system," which seems more in line with how I use the word *specialism* as a philosophy rather than simply a practice. From a business perspective, specialization is seen as an action, where special*ism* is a strategy of creating and leveraging your AUB *value*, not just another sales tactic.

While that may sound a little religious, I assure you I am agnostic when it comes to business practices and strategies. If it works, I believe in it. If it requires a "have faith" statement to get buy-in, I'm out.

What I have discovered in my research and practice over the last few decades is that the process of uniqueing your brand consistently produces dependably profitable results. In that way, specialism is the gravity beneath the feet of AUBs: relentless and immutable.

Generalist versus Specialist

So why does this generalist versus specialist brand identity occur in the first place? History has shown us that this evolution is inevitable. The specialist will always replace the generalist as a business sector or market matures.

A great example is the history of barbers, surgeons, and dentists. (Did you know they were related?)

> *Barber-surgeons were medical practitioners in medieval Europe who, unlike many doctors of the time, performed surgery, often on the war wounded. Barber-surgeons would normally learn their trade as an apprentice to a more experienced colleague. Many would have no formal learning, and were often illiterate.*

> *The red and white pole, which is still used to identify a barber's shop, was originally intended to reflect the blood and napkins used to clean up during bloodletting. This treatment was one of the main tasks of the barber-surgeon, as well as extracting teeth, performing enemas, selling medicines, performing surgery and, of course, cutting hair.* (Pelling, 1981)

Let's get crystal clear on this.

A **generalist** is a person whose knowledge, aptitudes, and skills are applied to a field as a whole or to a variety of different fields.

A **specialist** is any person who devotes him- or herself to one subject or branch of a subject or pursuit.

These perspectives become increasingly important when viewed through the lens of brand identity.

What (Exactly) Is an Authentically Unique Brand?

Authentic: (adj.) of undisputed origin or authorship; genuine: an authentic signature (Dictionary.com).

Unique: (adj.) having no like or equal; unparalleled; incomparable: The earliest meanings of unique when it entered English around the beginning of the 17th century were "single, sole" and "having no equal." By the mid-19th century unique had developed a wider meaning, "not typical, unusual," and it is in this wider sense that it means, "compared."

Brand: *(noun) the set of expectations, memories, stories and relationships that, taken together, account for a consumer's decision to choose one product or service over another* (Godin, 2009).

Rolling it back up into one idea, I define it this way:

Authentically Unique Brand (AUB): *(noun) a communication that relays the genuine essence of your unique story and/or purpose.*

AUBs are a central proof that entrepreneurs can use their purpose as the foundation for their strategic goals, marketing strategy, and competitive position.

Not only do AUBs define what makes entrepreneurs authentically happy (rather than just feeling good at the moment), they also attract customers who connect with that purpose, or at least the authenticity in presenting it as a core value. In psychological terms, this is known as *self-actualization.*

These AUBs don't occur in the wild. They are *created* when you choose the *who* and *what* of your business direction based on the *why* of you as a person or purpose. It's a simple idea that takes a lot of work to achieve.

Build a business on what makes you one-of-a-kind (your AUB), and you'll always work with people you love — and they'll love you right back.

AUBs aren't some newfangled form of marketing; they're a way for your tried-and-true marketing efforts to be more effective at drawing customers who will value you and your products and *want* to pay you more. (Experience has convinced me that paying more is the only way a customer can actually demonstrate how much they love you. I addressed the reasons for this in the chapter on Double Xs.)

After thirty years of creating Authentically Unique Brand identities and marketing strategies with worldwide clients from individual entrepreneurs to multimillion-dollar creative businesses, I've learned what works and what doesn't. With that experience, I have encapsulated those lessons here so that you, too, can discover how to create your own AUB and authentically attract your ideal clients by rising above the generalist noise.

Specialty or Commodity

An Authentically Unique Brand *win* is when you introduce your business in a way that takes a full advantage of your knowledge and experience and deliver it to clients who were previously overwhelmed by choice.

Your goal must be to help them define what they are looking for by clearly declaring what you are offering. Your intent must be enabling them to buy from you rather than selling to them. This is the future of success for creative and entrepreneurial businesses.

So what happens if you don't embrace specialism and continue to ride along the tracks of a generalized business? That answer is simple. You, your products, your services, and your brand identity will become *commoditized*.

In business, this term means a total lack of meaningful differentiation between similar products. Commoditized products have thin margins and are sold on the basis of price and not brand. This situation is characterized by standardized, ever cheaper, and common technology that invites more suppliers who lower the prices even further (BusinessDictionary.com).

Commoditization quickly forces you into a price war, which is a race to the bottom in which everyone is reduced to delivering similar products and services with the only differentiation being how low the price can be.

Finally, you may now be asking, what about *quality* as a differentiator? "Shouldn't the quality of my product or services matter more than anything else?"

Maybe it should — but it doesn't.

In the "Quality" chapter, I address this quality-as-differentiator myth in detail. For now, the simple answer is that your clients don't truly value the difference between good and great, which means you can't become great in their eyes using quality as an argument.

The true power of AUBs is being able to send a clear and personal message to your ideal client that will resonate deep within them and draw them to you, while simultaneously pushing away those you don't want to work with.

And the first step to that goal is defining the *who* of *you*.

Section 1: Brand Identity

Discovering the *who* of *you* is the key to creating your Authentically Unique Brand identity. Here, you will dig deep into what you are passionate about and how that represents the *why* and *who* of your life and work; then you'll make some tough decisions about the specialization niche you want to celebrate. You'll also examine ways to define your unique story in a few words and learn how to use those words to overpower your competition in the process.

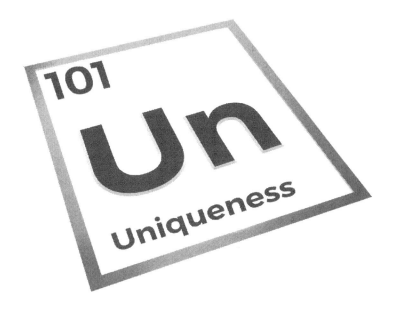

Element 101: Uniqueness

It is better to be one-of-a-kind than it is to be different.

The secret to long-term business and personal success is to choose the *who* and *why* of your message based entirely on what makes you unique.

In this world of over-promising, social networks, and blurry lines between friend and stranger, clients are more than ready to buy your *why* and *who* long before they buy *what* you do or even *how* you do it. So who are you?

What's in Your Soup?

For instance, if you were a soup, what kind of soup would you be? Like people, soups are complex and contain a myriad of ingredients, most of which are the same for everyone.

You could start by identifying some of the similar common categories.

Hot or cold soup?

Cream or water based?

Spicy or bland?

Vegetarian or omnivore?

And while all of these will help you categorize your soup, they aren't descriptive enough to define your soup's one-of-a-kind qualities.

When finding what defines you as unique, you face the same dilemma as the soup. To define yourself — rather than allowing others to define you — also means that you will have to make choices. *Hard* choices. You must decide what you want to be known for. To do that, you must identify a few attributes that exist within you and declare them as *iconic* for what you stand for.

They must represent you.

For example, let's imagine that multiple generations of your family have been working on the *perfect* **vegetable soup**, and yours is the best one yet!

Alas, even that declaration only positions you as ordinary if your only differentiating trait is tied to the quality of your ingredients or soup.

To be *extra*ordinary, you'll have to dig deeper. What *other* ingredients exist in your soup that give it unique character, even if they are so subtle that no one notices until you point them out?

Those subtle flavors are often the best kind of ingredients to talk about — the ones that nobody noticed until you brought attention to them, and afterward that is all they can think to taste.

Your soup probably has many smaller bits of spices, herbs, and flavorings that have been added over the years. And even though they are subtle, they remain important to the overall taste — or else they wouldn't need to be in there, right?

These can be the ingredients you define as *iconic* in that they become representative to what you want your soup (i.e., you) to stand for.

For the sake of illustration, let's imagine that in addition to the water, veggies, and general spices, there are also three other key ingredients that you have added: paper-thin slices of truffles, a splash of habanero pepper oil, and a dusting of dark-chocolate powder are all blended into your hot, soupy goodness.

It no longer makes sense to talk about the basic veggies or broth or spiciness, does it? It's now about the *other* things that you must now consciously elevate to become the iconic value proposition for your soup.

Now your message becomes the Chocolate Truffle with a Kick of Habanero Soup. This declaration will act as a magnet, both pulling the right customers toward you and pushing the wrong ones away.

In declaring this, you have effectively separated yourself from the general (i.e. boring) soup crowd. And did you notice that you didn't need to change a single thing in the soup (or yourself) to achieve this uniqueness? You were already putting in those unique ingredients, right? You just weren't shining a light on them.

This demonstrates how you don't need to *change* anything about you or your business to find your success in AUBs. Instead, you need only identify those things that you already possess as *extra*ordinary and bring them to the forefront of your brand message and identity.

Authenticity Words

Once you've discovered your own iconic attributes, you can use them in every communication to prospective clients, including business cards, your website, and especially as categories on your business blog. These are your **Authenticity Words**.

Not only are you declaring the value of these words that identify who you are, but you also begin to identify your own clients within these categories. Better yet, once you know these brand words, you can approach every marketing and sales opportunity with these words in mind.

Your Authenticity Words will bring more focus to how you present your value message and, thus, bring consistency to your brand and the mental imagery it invokes.

A side-note to consider: often, people think of the words *unique* and *different* as synonymous. This isn't true. And it's important to keep their differences in mind as your traverse this book.

Being *different* means you are not the same.

Being *unique* means you are one-of-a-kind.

Building an AUB on your one-of-a-kindness rather than your different-ness is powerful because no one can copy who you are, which means they can't even begin to compete with *you*.

Author's note: *I could (and may) write an entire book about the values of Authenticity Words and how to create them. For now, this and the additional information I reveal in the "Competition" chapter is enough to understand their value to AUBs and the chemistry of creating them. If you wish to learn more, there are many videos and recorded webinars posted on Authenticity Words at my website: jeffjochum.com.*

Element 102: Simplicity

Simple ideas are always the most powerful.

It has been said that achieving simplicity is never a simple task.

I define *simplicity* as the achievement of *authentic clarity*, where you can express your true meaning and purpose without any posturing or fakery and expect to be understood. I have discovered this requires a lot of effort.

In our current world, we assume that something is really important if it includes big words, complex descriptions, and difficult-to-understand concepts. Logically, we know this isn't true, yet we do it anyway.

Why do we allow this to word-bigness cloud our minds? In part, it is the result of what psychologists call *learned helplessness*. All intelligent animals, including humans, are wired to learn from their experiences, including experiences where they are baffled or confused. As a result, we become comfortable with confusion and have learned to accept it as the norm.

An example that demonstrates this point is where the bird raised in a cage will never fly, even when faced with the destruction of its cage—and certain death. Humans, raised on a constant diet of raw, complex data from a gaggle of sources will, over time, instinctively shut down their curiosity and decisiveness. In the same way the caged bird can't see flying as an option, people get used to assuming they cannot understand and, accordingly, stop seeking clarity.

Is it any wonder we've all become choice frozen?

This problem is never more evident than in how we have learned to communicate with each other in business. A primary failure-to-communicate problem is **e-mail**. We increasingly depend on our exchanges through e-mail, yet we find it increasingly impossible to read everything that comes in to our own inboxes.

On the other hand, we *illogically assume everything* we *send is being read.*

This logical disconnect only increases the irrationality and the complexity of how we see the problem of communication. And this in turn causes the paralysis by analysis that compounds the problem. The importance of expression has outpaced the importance of being understood.

Complexification

I define this problem as one of *complexification.* (Yes, I created this self-describing word.) We are choking on a diet of meaningless detail, ineffective marketing messages, and just too many metrics. Ironically, we think that we can solve this problem by increasing the use of statistical analysis (like demographics, junk-mail blockers, and spam algorithms) to determine which things we should and should not focus on.

Einstein gave us guidance on this when he said, "We cannot solve our problems with the same thinking we used when we created them". We should listen.

Where does this complexification come from? It is born in the heart of insecurity.

Psychologist John Collard at Yale University describes seven types of common fears, one of which is the "fear of thinking." Believing we are "unable to understand" allows for this fear. If we don't believe we have the power to solve a problem, then we can't be held responsible for it remaining unsolved.

I've spent many years working with businesspeople who lean on this I-can't-understand-so-its-not-my-fault approach to decision making ("Everyone would make the same decision as me if given the same data, so it really isn't my fault for making a bad decision!") and have never seen it produce anything but chaos. At best, it perpetuates the death by meeting syndrome. At worst, it is a cancer that spreads throughout an organization, having a zombie-like effect on decision-making.

Why does this happen?

More often than not, entrepreneurs are unsure of their value, untrained in their market, and unproven in their business, and this renders them unable to execute any long-term plan.

To succeed, people must have the freedom to be self-confident and the ability to be simple and clear. While precision matters when it comes to how others see you and how you see yourself, simple, clear, focused ideas are always the most potent.

From a marketing vantage point, the real challenge comes when we notice that people are simply blocking out this avalanche of information as a way to protect themselves against debilitating mental chaos. This makes the obstacle almost impossible to get past. As a rule, people are insecure and hate confusion, which is why it is so difficult to change even the most unfocused mind.

This is a problem that *Uniqueing Your Brand* solves.

Using an AUB, you get past these limitations of what is in our customers' minds; because we understand in detail why they act the way they do, starting with the mind's limitations. This is quite an achievement and feels like a daunting task when you realize that you can't change an irrational mind with rational arguments, as most marketing messages try to do. The best way to continue this success is to overcome these limitations and adopt a *need to know* approach when crafting your brand message.

A Need to Know

The military and intelligence communities have a guiding principle known as the *need to know* requirement.

Most people think this exists solely as a means to reduce the risk of secrets being leaked. Lesser known, and equally important, is that it also dramatically reduces the levels of *inaccuracy* that sneaks into information when it is passed from one person to another. By simply reducing the number of people who have the information in the first place, they can keep secrets both more confidential and more accurate.

Why should you care since you aren't trying to keep your product or service a secret? Because everything in our world is affected by the pull of chaos, including information. In an uncontrolled state, even the most valuable information will devolve into chaos, ultimately overwhelming the meaning of the information at its core.

The best example is the classic game of *telephone*, where a complex message is passed privately from one person to the next, with the group discovering at the end how dramatically the message changed while passing through the minds of everyone in the room.

And the success of this game doesn't always require a complex message to work. Even a *simple* message can get distorted dramatically as it passes from one person to the next… especially if it's boring.

People hate to be bored, so when they encounter a message that doesn't excite them, they either discard it (as they'd do outside the game) or enhance it (which they do when forced to relay a boring message). Either way, it's almost impossible to have the message arrive in its original form unless two circumstances are evident.

First, everyone in the game is actually *interested in the original information.* Then, and only then, can you assume the receipt of the message is interesting enough for them to hear, qualify, and retain.

Second, *the message is simple to understand and powerful enough to evoke a positive emotional response.* If these two criteria are met, those involved will regard the data as important and increase their efforts to maintain its accuracy.

AUBs leverage both of these criteria.

Authenticity Hates Complexity

Basically, people do not trust what they don't understand. In a nutshell, this is why marketing messages that promote AUBs succeed. Because they present a clear, simple message that resonates with similar people, they attract only those who are truly interested and—having gained the information you offer—happily grasp its value. This then enables them to relay it as a personal thought and idea instead of just a bit of miscellaneous data passing through them.

How simple is simple? It is most effective if you can declare *who* you are (i.e., what you stand for, your purpose, what you want to accomplish) in *ten words or fewer.*

Remember, your customers—and people in general—won't trust what they don't understand. And psychology and social sciences tell us that people have about a 7-10 word limit of what they can retain and understand, in the short term. So, ten words or less increases the chance that they will understand you, and therefore trust you.

That is critical because if they don't trust you, they won't buy from you.

One way to reinforce this is to craft a message that includes only what you need them to *remember* – as opposed to what you want them to know – and present it in the simplest way possible. We explore this thoroughly in the "Stickiness" chapter.

Element 103: **Stickiness**

Tell people only what you want them to remember.

How do we separate the things we want to remember from the things that we don't?

For instance, what pieces of data represents *information* rather than just random thoughts?

A definition of *information* is "something that reduces uncertainty," which means it must lead us to *understanding* something rather than just simply *knowing* it. It's not really information if you can't make sense of it or if it's badly timed.

Selling Food to Hungry People

In their book *What Sticks*, authors Rex Briggs and Greg Stuart write,

> *Another thing McDonald's learned through the research we conducted is what a big difference the time of day targeting makes: When you're trying to sell people food, it's best to advertise to them when they're hungry. Our research found that there's a four-hour window around lunchtime to show very appetizing images of food that can lead to a ten-point gain (from 36 percent to 46 percent!) on their intent-to-purchase measure than if advertised outside that lunchtime timeband. (2014)*

The point here is one of timing. Regardless of how authentic, clear, and well crafted your brand message is, it is only noise when it falls on customers who aren't interested.

So, how do you make them interested?

In truth, you can't *make* them do anything. The premise of *Uniqueing Your Brand* is the presentation of your amazing purpose and ideas, which compels prospective customers who already have, or are inclined to have, some interest — no matter how small — to lean in and hear your presentation.

Your brand message is designed to emotionally *elevate* customers' minds when they buy your products or services, not to *change* their minds. It helps to remember that they *want* to hear your message, meaning your marketing goal is to get it into their heads.

The challenge is that for you to be heard, they have to be *listening*.

To have any chance of accomplishing your mission, you have to get their attention. Otherwise, whatever you say won't stick. While there are many ways to get customers to see and hear you, none are more effective than storytelling.

Stories Are Sticky

Every TV advertising exec knows one basic rule about effectiveness: if you present a dozen features or benefits — even if each one is undeniably important — consumers won't recall *any* of them clearly.

For your Authentically Unique Brand message to be memorable and sticky, it must be simple. By *simple*, I mean not just being express in 10 words or less, but also having a *singular* focus. In addition to being short and sweet, it is equally important that you have a story that draws people in and connects with them at an emotional level.

You must be crystal clear on what your message says about you and your purpose and *only* deliver what you want clients to remember. How do you create these memorable stories? Here are a few building blocks.

Authenticity. How can you enable customers to believe in you? Sticky ideas have to carry their own authenticity. Generally, there isn't an external authority that can validate your message, which means your brand message has to vouch for you. To do that, your message must have *presumed credibility*.

As long as you can avoid complexificating the story, knowledge of details is a good indicator of credibility. For example, a story in which you can demonstrate your experience as an entrepreneur, and using simple, easy-to-understand real-world examples and vivid details will lend further authenticity to your AUB.

Additionally, if you feel that you can do it without introducing too much chaos into your story, you can also (lightly) weave one or two metrics and statistics into the story, for an added bump of authenticity.

Clarity. How do you ensure your AUB's purpose is clear? First, express your ideas with activities that include sensory information. This is where a lot of brand communication goes wrong. Mission statements, strategies, and visions are often ambiguous to the point of being meaningless.

Naturally sticky ideas take advantage of fully formed images (e.g., candy-apple-red sports cars, ear-piercing explosions, and the stench of overripe bananas) because our brains more easily remember multisensory items than bland product descriptions. Try to keep your AUB story rooted in the visceral energy that exists down deep inside you.

Sometimes, your AUB and story are big and it just isn't possible to encapsulate them into something as portable as 10 words or less. In that case, you can use *surprise*.

Surprise. One trick in keeping consumer interest when you need more time to get brand ideas across is to be counterintuitive and disrupt people's expectations. Surprise — and its side effect of increased focus — can be very effective in grabbing people's attention for short periods of time. For your brand message to endure, it must also ignite interest and curiosity.

A problem I personally have had is figuring out how to keep conference attendees engaged during the last hour of an all-day seminar.

To help with this, I use the Socratic method of teaching — asking questions that challenge the audience to make a decision. This leverages their curiosity and increases their awareness of what they don't yet know. Then we discover or define those answers together.

Finally, know that for people to take action, they have to *care*. *Passion* can help make that happen?

Passion. Most importantly, how do you get customers to actually *care* about your brand beliefs? To do that, you have to make them *feel* something. Note that we are wired to feel things for *people*, not for abstractions, like company visions or brand logos. People must to connect to what you believe in to have any chance at sparking an emotional response. Belief counts for a lot, but belief isn't enough.

How do you get people to care and *act* on your ideas? Tell stories. Golfers naturally swap stories after each game, and by doing so, enhance that experience. After years of exchanging stories, they have a richer, more complete mental catalog of critical situations they might confront during a game and the best solutions to those situations.

Research shows that mentally rehearsing a situation help us perform better when we encounter that situation in the physical environment. Similarly, hearing stories acts as a kind of mental video game, preparing us to respond more quickly and effectively.

The Information Paradox

Using a popular metaphor, one of our biggest challenges in getting your *why* and AUB across is distinguishing the "signal from the noise." And, you have to figure out how to do this without forcing your audience to consume *all* the noise, in the first place. To find that answer, we must consider only the perspective of the audience.

As a consumer of information, the big question is how we can we filter out data that we believe is unwanted by simply not allowing it in and/or not paying attention to it?

Sounds simple, but exactly how do we review it without actually reading it, first? Is there a first line of defense against the noise?

More directly stated, how can we know data is *important* if we don't actually consume and evaluate it? And worse, by evaluating it, aren't we raising it to a level of importance just by allowing it into our minds?

This problem is known as the *information paradox.*

We can overcome this paradox by applying a series of **five** information filters. Knowing these filters and how they effect your audience will help you to ensure your AUB gets into the brains of your potential customers and stays there.

The first filter is **categorical**; in which you can know the category or general type of incoming data by its initial source. For example, simply avoiding a *source* of very specific categorical material (e.g., *Sports Illustrated, The CPA Review,* or *National Lampoon*) filters out data that may hold no interest to you. Generally, your business niche will be used to create this polarization, pushing away those who have no need for your product or service in the first place.

The next level is non-categorical data like e-mail and general-topic periodicals that are a little harder to filter. This leads us to the second filtering method, which I refer to as a **summary** filter. By scanning the self-defined summary information in each collection of data (e.g., e-mail subject lines, periodical headlines, etc.), the consumer can choose to further engage this data – or not – in the hopes of encountering valuable and relevant information.

Moving on, if the data has successfully gotten through these initial two filters, it is more likely the recipient will then begin to actually consume (i.e., read it), and begin a serious search for the signal that resonates with them. At every sentence or idea they encounter, they start applying an **advocate** filter, where they'll *continue* to consume the data as long as it feeds their belief that they'll ultimately benefit from the information.

Once they've completed the consumption of the data and defined it as *information* (remember, that is "something that reduces uncertainty"), the next gatekeeper is the all-important **evangelist** filter, in which they determine if this information important enough to retain in their limited memory banks in hopes of deriving future value through situational application or sharing (i.e., evangelizing) with others.

Quick summary: Our goal has been to tell someone something through data, and at this point we could consider our efforts a success, even though one final filter has yet to be engaged. For the sake of the AUB, this is the most important filter to know.

That is the **true believer** filter and lives at the top of our information pyramid. At this point, not only does our audience understand the information, but they have also *connected* it in some way at an emotional level of their personality. As a result of knowing this information, they may feel compelled to make changes in themselves and in the world around them. As you might assume, this achievement is the holy grail of marketing.

It is also the expected result of an AUB.

In psychological terms, getting customers to react in this way is another form of self-actualization. In all cases, the purpose of these data filters is to help them avoid, limit their exposure to, or simply not retain unfiltered data that has little or no chance of moving to the status of valuable information in their minds.

We know they simply do not have room in their minds, or in their lives, to store useless data.

Ensure you are focused on presenting something that gets past each of the gatekeepers and resonates with the essence of your prospective customers, and you'll have discovered the first (big!) step toward building an army of evangelists — true believers in what you stand for and in your business.

Element 104: **Better**

You must be different from better to be great.

One of the first homework exercises I give to my entrepreneur students is to have them interview a few of their favorite clients to discover why their customers hired, or bought from them, in the first place.

Initially, everyone offers up three reasons.

1. You, or your business message, made them feel *comfortable*. (Meaning that your basic business persona and your client's personality didn't clash.)
2. Your brand is *attractive*. (Often meaning that your website and/or other advertising weren't obviously bad and that you seemed consistent in your style.)
3. You acted *professional*. (Meaning dependable — they assumed you had more to gain by delivering the promised product than by acting irresponsibly.)

Combined, these responses are called the *trust promise*.

While all these points may be true and important, they are not really tied to your AUB, since *every* happy customer says these same three things. If any one of them is missing, you have an unhappy customer.

What is important is the *fourth* thing: the reason they chose you over everyone or everything else. Assume correctly that everyone can deliver on that trust promise; and the power of your AUB begins to take on more importance. This fourth factor is tied back to your Authenticity Words and ultimately is what makes you **better** (often seen as **best**) in the client's mind.

Different from Better

The thing that will always elevate you above the masses of good is having genuine insight into who you are and why you are that way and being able to relay that to your prospective clients.

This is best delivered with transparent authenticity and is the main ingredient in the formula that will declare you as an AUB.

This transparent declaration helps your customers connect to you and reassures them that you can make them happy. The happier they are as a result of your product or service, the *better* (i.e. more valued) you are in their minds.

Everything you say and do must reinforce your AUB and create a compelling reason for clients to want to *support*, not just buy from, you and your business. The real trick is to be able to discard the snappy, useless slogan in favor of the important points of your AUB value proposition. To better understand this, let me describe one of my personal experiences in creating a purpose-based message that possessed the ability to both speak the company's intent and draw customers to it.

The World's Best Entrepreneurs

The year was 2004, and I was hired to help a business-to-business (B2B) company that had been around for about three years with reasonable success selling à la Carte products to professional-service entrepreneurs. My job was to find a way to drive them upward into a quickly growing market with the intent of capturing the lion's share of that small-business entrepreneurs' market.

I understood the inflated value of exclusivity and connection to that market segment, so the first thing I did was create a private, exclusive community where this widely distributed and isolated group of professionals could gather, both personally and virtually, and feel as if they were part of something larger than themselves.

To monetize this as well as create a sense of the elite belonging, I also added a hefty subscription component to the company's services, thereby retiring the unruly and chaotic à la carte system that had been in place since the company's inception in favor of a more elite, exclusive option.

The real challenge was to figure out how to get entrepreneurs to join the community and begin paying subscription fees for products and services that they had previously enjoyed at zero cost. I knew that some form of rebranding would be necessary and wanted to make sure that it projected our newly crafted AUB strategy of "We all succeed together—or not at all."

To determine whether the team could create an effectively *exclusive* message for this new company model, I did a deep-dive analysis of the company, leaving no stone unturned while looking for anything that it possessed that its competitors could not easily copy. Among many other discoveries, I noticed that we had already recruited and gained the loyalty of a few well-respected trust leaders who seemed willing to promote themselves—and the company—within this marketplace.

While there weren't many of these advocates at the time, we definitely had more than any competitor had. This made ours the best of the best. I chose to create a strategy campaign and national tour as a forum for these respected thought leaders to sing their praises— and ours, of course—with the added declaration that we were now the company that was "Trusted by the World's Best Entrepreneurs."

The response was immediate and overwhelming. In less than one year, the company more than tripled its user base (now paying an average of $200 a month for services they had previously gotten for free), and in just over two years, had gone from less than $10 million in revenue to almost $40 million. The company was sold to famed equity buyout company Apax Partners in 2006 for a sizeable return.

Was the "world's best" message really the only key differentiator in elevating us above all other competitors in that crowded space?

Of course!

Maybe.

Who knows?

It's hard to narrow down the full causal effectiveness of a message like that.

What I do know is that it *defined* us as a community as well as a company. Inside and out, everyone felt compelled to make this "trusted by the best" message *true*. Every. Single. Day. Employees, customers, and even vendor partners all marched with this banner held high.

In the end, it was a self-fulfilling prophecy—as all good messages should be—and our customers knew that just being part of the community elevated them to the ranks of "world's best." Our customers defined themselves through their association with the uniquely "better" community that we had offered, and they were better for it.

Element 105: Quality

Quality won't differentiate or elevate your value.

For twenty years, Ford Motor Company tried to differentiate itself from competitors by claiming they were focused on quality. You may remember their slogan: "Quality is Job One."

By declaring this as their first priority, they assumed the American public would choose Ford cars over competitors not based on style or something they could see, but on something they were told exists inside their vehicles.

This was a failure.

The reason this strategy was unsuccessful for Ford was because no one really knows how to gauge the quality of a complex product like an automobile, except maybe automobile engineers.

For their campaign to work, they would have needed to educate the public to the technical level of an automobile engineer and then convince everyone that Ford vehicles were technically better than all the others in every one of their categories.

Ford learned the hard way that while quality may be necessary for a product to work, it would never be the priority for customers to buy it.

What is their customer's priority? Experience, of course.

"It Works!"

Quality used to be something we could measure by workmanship, raw materials, years of experience, or even skill of production. Those days are gone.

When labels went from the inside of our jeans to the outside, quality started being about **who we are** and not how the jeans were manufactured.

Dr. Clotaire Rapaille is a leading expert in cultural anthropology who spent decades studying behaviors, and he writes about **quality** in his book *The Culture Code*:

The very first imprint for quality for many of us is a negative one. It comes when something doesn't do what it is supposed to do. The child's game quits; the computer crashes; the dishwasher turns the repair man into a family member. Our positive imprints regarding quality focus on functionality rather than the brilliance of the design or the excellence of its performance. The remote control requires one to be in a specific place, but at least it changes the channels. The clock radio isn't much of a radio, but it's a reliable clock. The car doesn't have luxurious amenities, but it keeps on moving…The culture code for quality in America is IT WORKS. (2006)

To summarize, since our clients always assume that whatever we deliver will work, quality is only relevant when it *doesn't* work.

Something We Can Lose and Never Gain

I am *not* saying that you are free to deliver awful products and/or services to customers, and they won't be able to tell the difference between good and bad.

Quite the opposite.

Thanks to the broadening education the Internet has given us, everyone now seems to inherently know the difference between *good* and *bad*. Where the challenge comes in is helping them understand the difference between good and *great*. And this cannot be done using the concept of quality.

Customers assume **all** products in today's market *work* (i.e., are "good enough"), just like basic respect and knowing your customer are also assumed as universal expectations, not something special that only a few can deliver. Entrepreneurs often make this mistake by tying their value to something that their clients can't see — like the technical skill behind the creation of a product.

Going back to Ford, they learned the hard way that how a car makes us *feel* is more important than how it's made. In the same way, great products will never make up for a bad experience. And a great experience will always make up for mediocre products. If your clients love you, they love your products. If they don't, you can be the greatest producer in the world, and it won't matter.

A Transformation Story: Jennifer Chaney

At the start of 2011, I found myself at a crossroads. I had just finished my taxes for the previous year and was literally in tears. In my work as a professional service provider, my sixty-plus-hour workweeks, ridiculously late nights, and countless weekends spent with other people's families had translated into a whopping $15,000 after taxes and expenses.

Why had I worked so hard for so little money?

When all was said and done, I was making roughly fifteen dollars an hour!

Good grief! I paid my housecleaner seventeen dollars an hour! I knew instantly that this was not worth all of the hours I was forced away from my family — both physically and emotionally. At that time, I had two young kids at home and was sadly missing their childhood. And for what? Low pay? High risk? Hit-or-miss customer wins?

I knew I had to make a big decision. Was I going to keep going at this pace, risk the happiness of my family, and cross my fingers that things would change? Or would I call it quits, take my toys, and go home?

It isn't so easy to quit, though.

Like so many entrepreneurs, I couldn't wrap my head around the idea of quitting — not after how hard I had worked and with the possibilities I still imagined lay before me. No one would have faulted me for packing it all up, but I decided that I was going to figure out how to do it right. Then, if I was still unsatisfied with the results, I could walk away without regret or second thoughts.

As fate would have it, I had recently heard Jeff speak about unique brand marketing and knew this was the right idea for me at the right time. I joined a coaching group he was forming and began the efforts of discovery, the first step in his process. I was able to step back and take a long look at my business from a totally different perspective. I stopped focusing on the money itself and took a very thorough look at who I was and whom I wanted as clients.

We started out by examining my existing clients.

To my surprise, when I sat down with my client list and started reading over the names, I saw an emotional pattern emerge. The clients I had the best time with, the ones I *loved* working with, were people I could easily have a margarita with — *they were a lot like me*. The rest of my clients had actually caused me some amount of sorrow; they were the ones that I couldn't imagine having to endure a cup of coffee with, much less a cocktail!

How had I not noticed this before? It seemed painfully obvious as I looked at my customer list. I realized that the ones I *really* loved were the clients who hired me to come into their homes and celebrate the bright spots in their seemingly crazy world.

Everything about these awesome clients brought me joy — *true* joy. From phone calls to e-mails to asking for payment, I was at ease with them.

And it was with this realization that a new Jennifer Chaney business was born.

Fast-forward through two years of ongoing discovery, definition, and declaration, and I am now working happily, every day. My life and my business don't conflict any longer because I don't feel the pressure to take *every single customer*. Now I only take the ones that I *want* to, and I easily say, "No, thank you" to the ones I can tell won't bring me joy. I am in control for the first time since 2006.

My business no longer runs me; I run it.

Authentically Unique Branding gives me power and confidence — a clear desire, message, and goal. It allows me to focus and be who I am with families who are like me. This is powerful. Amazingly and overwhelmingly powerful. I feel blessed. And it all started by choosing to make a change.

Once I felt the power of choosing *one thing* and doing it really well, I can't ever imagine going back to the way things used to be. And certainly not for fifteen dollars an hour.

Section 2: Brand Value

With the baseline of your authentic *who* as a foundation, we now begin to develop how your clients experience you. With an eye toward creating ways to easily declare the differences that make you special, you will explore the concepts of comparison, quality, and authenticity, which live at the heart of everything you will say and do from this point forward.

Element 201: **Competition**

Competing against "bad" will never make you "great" in the minds of customers.

I never personally met Charlie Brown Scarborough, though I feel like I know him pretty well.

Charlie was an Authentically Unique Brand icon, and I suspect he never knew it. He embraced the principles of specialism at his core and enabled his business to be a clear reflection of the power of personal differentiation.

Charlie was a plumber in Georgia. And he whistled while he worked. Here's a review of Charlie's work that I found on Angie's List:

> *The guy came by about 5 p.m. yesterday and was super nice. Feeling a little strange leaving a stranger alone in my bedroom, I stuck close by. This guy cracked me up because the whole time he was working, he whistled — and was actually pretty good at it. He seemed to be a fan of Harry Connick/Michael Bublé type music. Normally whistlers bug me, but he was entertaining.*

OK, but, did he fix the faucet? Of *course* he did! If he hadn't, this review would've been about an incompetent plumber who spent more time whistling than doing his job. And what if he hadn't whistled while he worked? We wouldn't be reading this nice comment because "doing your job" never really gets any praise.

Let me repeat: *just* **doing your job never gets praised.**

Overcoming that fact elevated him to the top of his profession, as well as to the top of the minds of many customers. As the "whistling plumber," he was an easier choice than the thousands of other general plumbers in Atlanta.

If I have to hire a plumber, he or she may as well entertain me while they're working, right?

So, how *do* you get the praise you deserve?

84

First, you must ensure you teach the customer exactly what you want praise for. The most effective way to address this is with the Authenticity Words discussed (briefly) in the "Uniqueness" chapter.

The following is some direction on how to create effective Authenticity Words — and what to avoid.

The Test of Opposites

By embracing your AUB, you elevate *who* you are and *why* you do it over *what* you do or *how* you do it. And as we've seen in the previous examples, generalist strategies and tactics are limited to running a race. Specialism isn't restricted by this limitation. By creating an AUB differentiator based on the why and who of you, you make it impossible for any competitors to even enter the race in the first place. This lets you create your own race — one that *only you* can win.

To do that, you will need to clearly define your Authenticity Words to represent you. **These are not slogans or taglines.** Rather, they are simple, authentic single words that you feel declare what is at the center of you and your business. They must be strong, clear, and unambiguous.

To test the strength of your Authenticity Words, the first step is choosing ones with opposite definitions that aren't negative. For example, the word *trust* doesn't work because the opposite is *untrustworthy*, which no competitor would ever claim. Alternately, *natural* is a word that is unambiguous. Its opposite is *refined*, which is equally clear without being negative.

Here are some other examples of words that don't work and words that do.

Words That Don't Work:

- trusted (vs. untrustworthy)
- authentic (vs. fake)
- passionate (vs. disinterested)

Words That Do Work:

- modern (vs. old-fashioned)
- bold (vs. subtle)
- natural (vs. refined)

When your Authenticity Words are genuine and stand up to the test of opposites, they become the pillars of your business message and what you stand for.

Winning without Competing

I think the most common metaphor for business must be "the race." It enables us to compete by staying focused on the finish line (if we have actually defined our finish line) while still expecting all kinds of disruptions, both known and unknown, along the way. One of the premises of this viewpoint is how we define our preparation for the race.

In the normal course of planning, businesses largely use three steps to completion and, presumably, success. These three steps are: define *goals*, select *strategies,* and develop *tactics.* One of the most common problems among small-business owners is jumping past goals and moving straight to tactics or strategies, thinking immediate action will get them to the finish line faster.

The problem with that logic is that the primary mission of tactics is to keep up a fast pace for the longest period of time. That is, it's assumed that if you have deeper resources, better stamina, and stronger legs, then you will be better than any of the competition that was foolish enough to compete with you. However, tactics are useless when they aren't being driven by a clear strategy.

Unlike tactics, strategy focuses on preparation as well as overall performance and how to improve it, even before the race has begun. For example, if I decided to compete in an Ironman triathlon (swimming, running, and biking), there are multiple strategic options to increase my chances of winning.

Strategy #1: I could acknowledge that swimming is my weakest skill of the three and decide to spend more time training in the pool in hopes of bringing up my swim scores.

Strategy #2: I could decide to focus on my strongest skill in the hopes that driving myself to the top of that performance pyramid will offset my lousy swimming scores—assuming they didn't get any worse.

Sadly, even the best strategies can't be effective if you don't have clear and concise goals for the race in the first place.

A goal is a *finish line*. Note I said *a* rather than *the* finish line. Like the Ironman, your overall business "race" is most likely a series of smaller, ongoing competitions.

For you, those individual races may look like this:

- Finding new clients
- Keeping existing ones
- Lowering your costs
- Raising your perceived value

All of these are really goals in themselves, each with its own set of strategies and tactics and each moving you closer to a general sense of security, satisfaction, and success.

However, focusing on tactics and strategies before you have a goal can be deceptive, because engaging in tactics and strategies requires activity that makes you feel like you are making progress, even when you are not. The biggest failure for an entrepreneur occurs when his or her overall goal is undefined or unclear.

The value of a well-defined and achievable goal cannot be understated. Without it, you will not only see success slip away, but you will also be stuck in a never-ending struggle to determine where you are on the racetrack and how well you are doing.

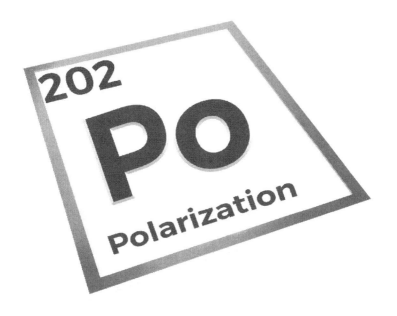

Element 202: Polarization

To be trusted, you must risk being unloved.

Companies that want everyone to buy from them lose focus and eventually suffer a dire fate.

Due to the fast pace of today's marketing environment, the danger of losing a market position or suffering from unseen disruption is great. Staying focused is the best tool to avoid that disruption.

Yet, most businesses are willing to forfeit that focus to ensure they are not creating any detractors in the marketplace. This fear of potential negativity has a more disruptive result than the one they were trying to avoid.

By remaining narrowly focused, you can polarize consumers into two distinct groups: those who support you and those who don't. As I mentioned earlier, Double X consumers love this kind of elite association and expect you to remain narrowly focused and carve out a strong niche, with solid brand recognition. Let me illustrate this with a real-world example.

Demonizing Your Competition

In 2006, a company I was advising on their marketing strategy arrived at a huge industry conference only to find that a new, powerful competitor had also arrived on the scene. A quick competitive review revealed that this new rival was superior in almost every way to what my client was offering at the time. There was no way they could compete head to head without at least one year of additional development.

My job was to find a way to keep this competitor at bay for (at least) the one year needed to catch up.

As luck would have it, this new competitor made a critical strategic error, and made my task incredibly easy. Rather than creating a focused Authentic Unique

Brand, as we had done, they had opted to be *all* things to *all* customers, without any preference of one niche over another.

This was the fatal flaw I could leverage.

Once I noticed this *generalist* position, I trained all of the sales people to openly praise this new competitor as the "best company in the *home-office* market," which was the niche I knew had the smallest customer-based and revenues. I knew *positioning* them there would polarize and repel the larger, non-home-office market from using them as that market had shown itself to be very isolated.

The result was that this competitor was never able to get a foothold of trust in the larger marketplace, and within a year, they had disappeared from the landscape, in large part because they had been unable to decide on a singular focused strategy.

Consumers are suspicious of indecisive companies.

Their suspicions are often justified because products or services from companies that are unfocused are rarely as good as those from niche companies.

Uniqueing Your Brand is a way of concentrating on one idea that defines what you stand for in the minds of your customers. Having that strong AUB identity will always give you an advantage over your generalist competitors.

For most businesses, especially small entrepreneurial ones, it makes a lot more sense to market a single successful product or service to one dedicated group of people.

One way to stay ahead of the tendency toward chaos as your business grows, and to keep your business focused, is keep your personal goals in mind and not get sucked into competition with others when you reach a plateau.

Staying focused on delivering your consumer promise and remaining true to the purpose of your company will always help keep you on track.

Remind yourself of your Authenticity Words every day.

Keep them in front of you. Write them on a sticky note and post it on your computer monitor. Post them on your bathroom mirror. Keep your focus, and you won't drown in competitive anxiety.

Love Your Enemies

Every good idea has at least one enemy. The bigger the enemy, the better the opportunity. Specialism's primary enemy is generalization. Jack-of-all-trade companies hate specialists. They represent the future and, even worse, are delivering the "death by a thousand cuts" that defeats most generalist companies. That's good!

Controversy is not a bad thing; don't be afraid of it.

Rather, it is a powerful tool that you can use to drive your message into the minds of consumers. Exploit it. People are drawn to strong, absolute positions and statements. The more clearly you deliver your message, the more valuable it will be for creating buzz in your market.

In fact, the best way to create buzz is by taking a position that polarizes some other group or market segment (without being negative or demeaning, of course) and therefore evokes a strong response.

With social networks like Facebook, Instagram, and Pinterest exploding in the consumer's world, buzz is one of the least expensive and more effective means of getting your business noticed.

However, make no mistake; buzz is *not* the message — it's only the delivery method.

Without a clear, authentic statement of what you stand for and how you specialize, you'll never build the idea-bomb that you're hoping the buzz will detonate.

Element 203: Imperfection

The fastest way to create trust is by revealing non-critical imperfections.

I trust the BBC more than I trust NBC (or CBS or ABC or FOX). Why? It isn't as polished and perfect as its American counterparts.

The BBC doesn't use flashy logos and graphic fireworks for every news story, nor does its newscasters appear perfectly coifed or manufactured.

As a result, when they give me the news, it feels like *the truth*. I don't actually know if the BBC's lack of sophistication is more truthful than other networks. In fact, it seems I trust them more *because* of their reporting imperfections, not in spite of them.

In our minds, being imperfect creates a sense of authenticity and, with it, **trust**. In any business where trust is a critical factor to success (like yours), these imperfections are the most powerful ways for you to create trust in your clients.

Note that these must be *noncritical* imperfections. If newscasters couldn't articulate the story or simply made stuff up as they went along or were openly intoxicated, no amount of authentic imperfection would cross the resulting chasm of distrust.

The point is that there's no need to work hard on being perfect. In fact, your imperfections will create more trust in your relationships with your clients and prospects because imperfections make us more human.

And it's your humanity that people truly trust.

One of the best examples to demonstrate this is when fellow writer and Disney TV personality Me Ra Koh was being interviewed by Sony for a strategic partnership in 2006. (Her transformation story is included following Section 3.)

At the end of Sony's impressive presentation about how their combined brands could be valuable to each other, Me Ra slowly raised her hand and said, "May I ask a question?"

"Sure," said the VP in charge, while the other half-dozen suits around the mahogany table nodded enthusiastically. Me Ra looked around the room slowly and then straight into the eyes of the VP.

"I want to represent Sony with the utmost respect and integrity," she started, "and that brings me to a question."

"Please, go ahead, Me Ra," replied the VP in charge, "ask anything."

"OK. Did you know I was a patient in a psychiatric ward, many years ago?" she asked, without taking her eyes from him. (I'm told her husband moaned audibly at this point.)

Following five seconds of silence, the VP leaned toward Me Ra and smiled. "Yes, of course we knew that already, Me Ra. In fact, we think the world is hungry for someone who represents transparent authenticity with such integrity."

Wow.

I've asked her since why she felt compelled to bring it up at that time and whether she did so because she was afraid they would discover it later. She replied, "Not at all. It is just who I am, and that's what they said they wanted." I think this is a prime example of how fearlessly embracing and sharing your imperfections with those you want to create a relationship with will always establish a level of trust that can't be acquired any other way.

Guilty Pleasures Will Set You Free

As you can see, transparency is a pillar of the AUB philosophy. Your business position and goals need to align with who you are so that you can be yourself every single day and, in doing so, meet your clients' expectations — and your own.

So how do we create trust in your prospects and clients?

Be vulnerable.

In the first chapter of her book *Daring Greatly*, Brené Brown shares her perception that many people today are struggling with the belief that they are not good enough to be worthy of love and connection. In fact, she says, this collective belief is so strong that it is actually reshaping our culture to see vulnerability as a weakness instead of strength (Brown, 2012).

Like Ms. Brown, I believe the willingness to acknowledge and act on painful, uncomfortable, or frightening feelings is an act of bravery. Inside our heads, vulnerability is not just associated with negative emotions. It is also where love, empathy, creativity, and trust originate.

Being vulnerable doesn't mean you have to perform an act of self-effacing embarrassment. However, it does mean that you must show your noncritical weaknesses (those that don't create permanent, negative results) in a way that triggers a customer's empathy and demonstrates the authenticity of your personality.

One way to accomplish this is by revealing some *guilty pleasures* in your biography or online persona. This has the marvelous effect of connecting with the indulgences of others who share your attributes and establishes you as trustworthy and authentic in customers' minds.

This can be seen in the online bios of some very successful and happy AUB entrepreneurs. For example, TJ Romero is a wedding photographer in Denver, Colorado, who specializes in brides who are "nostalgic and romantic and love the idea of a handcrafted wedding."

In addition to being a romantic nostalgic, he's also young, funny, and a little brash, and he wants his prospective customers to see *that* when they read his online bio at **http://tjromerowedding.photography**.

Here are a few samples:

- Sometimes, I hire housecleaners while Lisa is at work, and take the credit.

- Whenever Lisa goes to sleep early, I eat the stash of ice cream hidden in the back of the freezer.

- After running out of sugar at home, I grab handfuls from the condiment bar at Starbucks and stuff them in my pockets.

Each of these bullets says something about TJ—something raw and unfiltered. He has empowered you to truly know him in just a few short lines.

And these guilty pleasures reveal his vulnerability and draw you, and his prospective clients, in. Does it make you like him? Sure it does, if you share his quirkiness. In fact, it doesn't matter whether you like him based on these revelations. His intent was for you to *know* the authentic person. From this revealing self-portrait, you do, and that creates trust.

Another great example is self-described troublemaker Tracy Moore, a self-defined "tornado of energy" who is now working to build confidence in high-school-aged girls in Billings, Montana. Her bio reveals more than a little about what you can expect if you work with her.

- To me, a no trespassing sign means it's probably an awesome location to hang out.

- I also believe a roped off slope on the mountain means there's more powder for me and I don't have to share.

- One of my dreams is to cage dive with great white sharks. I want to look one straight in the eye.

- I always love a good prank, whether I'm the one getting pranked or doing the pranking.

In both of these examples, and with the many other businesses that I have helped to unique their brands, the imperfections revealed to prospective clients become compelling reasons to lean into — or run away from — the business. Both are *big* wins, since the whole idea of AUB success is to do exactly that.

Element 204: Signatures

People trust people before they trust companies or brands.

Connecting your AUB to your name adds great credibility.

It also reduces the perceived risk of doing business with you, and in the noisy world of business messaging, nothing ties more closely to your *who* than your name.

Naming Your Rose

Shakespeare would have us believe that a rose by any other name would still smell as sweet. I hate to disagree with The Bard, but I believe that if it had been named the "thorny skin-ripper," he most likely would never have written about it in the first place. And it certainly would have a much smaller audience sniffing at its sweet-smelling petals.

In the world of Authentically Unique Brands, the name you choose for your product or service is probably the single most important decision you can make, because — like the example above — it had better focus clearly on the value and purpose you want your consumer to be drawn to.

In the case of entrepreneurial businesses, nothing is stronger than your own name.

Surprisingly, this idea of intentionally naming your company after yourself, or using some form of descriptive moniker, is one of the most controversial ideas I've advocated over the years. For some reason, people are as infatuated with the naming process as they seem to be with the creation of a logo design (which also amazes me). My advice to everyone is to overcome this fascination and stick to what works.

I contend that no one ever got the job — or lost it — because of a creative company name or logo or tagline.

These things are designed to enhance your primary AUB, not define it.

If brands are as trustworthy as personal names, then why does Sergei Brin (cofounder of Google) still have to sign his name on the company's contracts, rather than just scribbling "Google" on the bottom line?

Because without a name, we don't trust his promise.

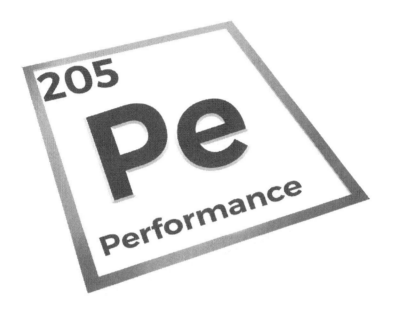

Element 205: Performance

Customer experience is a performance art.

Jennifer Goldberg Rozenbaum is a very successful photographer who focuses exclusively on working with women who want to celebrate their "fearless femininity."

She does this through a personal experience in her Long Island, New York studio. An incredibly skilled and experienced photographer, she consistently produces beautiful images for every client (of course!)

She also understands her images are not nearly as valuable as the experience itself. This is why Jen works very hard to be a *performance artist*, even though her *job* is to take pictures. Taken directly from her site (**http://jenerations.com**) even a small bit of her online bio tells the story of that focus on experience.

- *The true power of a woman can never be taken away by sweatpants.*
- *For me, putting on lip-gloss is like Clark Kent taking off his glasses.*
- *When playing truth or dare, always choose dare.*
- *I believe the scale doesn't measure your worth. (Besides it's usually lying, anyway).*
- *You can own your world if you live fearlessly, think audaciously and act spontaneously.*

Performance versus Product Business Models

Production art produces a result wherein knowledge of the artist is unnecessary to the buyer's appreciation of it. You can see a painting or sculpture or read a novel and love it without knowing anything about how it was produced or whom the artist was.

Performance art is the opposite. The bulk of the client's appreciation is linked directly to his or her experience of the creation process. Continuing with the professional photography example, it has evolved into a performance art because clients who love their photographer love their images even more than ones who don't. (In fact, I'm not sure there ever was a client who loved the images and not the photographer.)

A Transformation Story: ShootDotEdit.com

When we first started ShootDotEdit, our goal was to provide our services to every creative business across the globe. It shouldn't matter how you expressed your creativity or what niche you had chosen for yourself—you were our prospective client! We knew that would require a lot of effort and resources, but we were up to the challenge—or so we thought!

The initial good news is that we accomplished much of our goal rather quickly. Before we knew it, entrepreneurs from all over the globe were sending us work requests, and we said *yes* to everyone! It wasn't long before this yes-to-everything strategy started to drag us down.

The problem had become how to address thousands of differing requests. Every project required a different type of result, different customer-service requirements, different turnaround times, and even different price points.

Just as quickly as we had skyrocketed up, we became overwhelmed with the impossible task of being "right" for every different project and keeping every project manager happy—all while staying profitable under the pressure of competition.

Ah, profitability. The irony is that as a reward for being innovative and creating a new business sector, competitors were now popping up left and right and competing with us in the only way they knew—price.

Using price as our primary value proposition, we had gotten stuck in a race to the bottom and knew bankruptcy is often the only prize for "winning" a low-price race. Not only had it gotten harder to keep our wide array of clients happy, but it was also getting harder to stay profitable.

The idea of specialism and Authentically Unique Brands was introduced to us in July 2010. Frankly, we had a hard time believing this was *the idea* to solve our problems. How defocusing away from a chunk of our existing market make us a better company, make our clients happier, and generate more profits? The logic of less equaling more was hard to buy into, at first.

As we progressed through the process described in this book, it began to make sense.

We came from a niche industry; in fact, that experience was how we discovered the market demand and what really made us special in the first place. So why not focus on other companies with the same specialized need? We could build our entire brand message on what we knew best!

And, we did.

In three short years, we grew from struggling start-up to market leader—living at top of a pyramid that we had invented. It wasn't easy. Lots of tough choices came at us relentlessly as we went through the process of creating an AUB. But, we pushed onward and now our brand message is relatively bulletproof. Best of all, our decision-making skills are also topflight.

The true benefits of our AUB, though, were much more far reaching. Yes, we were able to service our very special customer, making us much more optimized and streamlined. But by declaring what we were all about (and likewise, what we weren't about), we attracted the *best* in our market. Because our brand message is so clear and authentic, we are able to price at the top of the market and be seen as the best of the best.

In the end, AUB creation was a shift in the model that affected every part of our business. Our brand benefited from the clientele we attracted.

Our operations benefited from the singular type of client. Our customers always knew exactly whom they were talking to. And, best of all, we enjoyed true focus.

Now we always know whom we are working for, what they want, and how to meet their needs. AUB's primary benefits — clarity and focus — allowed us to grow at rocket speeds. And that takes us right back to our original goal.

Section 3: Brand Execution

The first two sections represented a large percentage of the mental heavy lifting in the Authentically Unique Brand journey by motivating you to explore your uniqueness and differentiate based on those discoveries. Now it is time to make some hard choices, risk being unloved, and know the difference between wasting time and wasting customer trust.

Element 301: **Choices**

Choosing is a hard, emotional process that can't be controlled by logical arguments.

Over the years, I have found that the ability to be decisive, especially when there isn't enough data, is the true separator of the sustainable successes from the generally unsuccessful (or once-lucky).

As I mentioned earlier in this book, this ties back to one of Trout and Ries's 22 *Immutable Laws of Marketing*: **The Law of Sacrifice:** where you have to give up something in order to get something.

When you make a decision to do something (anything), you are also choosing to *not focus on everything else.*

The anxiety of *missing* all those potentially great opportunities can be overwhelming. I advise you not to worry about whether it's always the *right* choice as long as it is the best choice for *you*. Every successful business leader I've ever known shares a similar motto:

I'd rather make a controversial decision quickly than have someone else make the "right" one for me because I dawdled.

When people are insecure, they often look to others to help them make decisions. The assumption is that others have superior taste or knowledge or experience and that following someone else's lead will somehow give us the value of those things without having to gain them ourselves.

This is one reason the bandwagon strategy of using terms like "best-selling" or "fastest-growing" has positive effects on the consumer. However, as I mentioned earlier, this method of using herd mentality through generalized endorsement is losing effectiveness and is being replaced by a much higher-touch, socially connected endorsement.

Customers Lie

When queried, customers will usually tell you that "more choices" would motivate them to "buy more." On the surface that logic sounds correct. It isn't.

The more choices you offer them; the more business you are losing.

It's well documented that when you give people too many choices, they just stop buying. Known as *choice paralysis*, it is a common problem in marketing strategies.

Entrepreneurs, like most small-business owners, mistakenly believe that customers want choice because that is what they *said* they want. Unfortunately, research shows there is a gap between what people say they want and what actually makes them happy about their decisions.

While giving the customer choices may make them feel temporarily powerful, ultimately they are more likely to suffer from confusion anxiety and buyer's remorse.

So what is the best solution? Suggest (as personally as you can) the most common choice while offering some level of customization — even if the details must remain undefined until they choose it. For example, using phrases like "most popular" or "best-selling" has the power to reduce customer anxiety while not taking away the choices available to them.

This is not a new behavior, by the way. Legend has it that when Henry Ford was asked if he did any "market testing" before he created the automobile, he allegedly replied, "Absolutely not. If I'd asked what they want, they'd have told me 'a faster horse.'"

And while I rarely feel the need to quote Steve Jobs, in this case, I think it is appropriate. His basic consumer mind-set can be distilled to this statement: "People don't know what they want until you show it to them" (Jobs, 1998).

Why People Buy

There has always been a lot of discussion and speculation about why people buy what they buy and when. I covered a lot of this motivation in "The Big Lie" chapter.

We now know that asking your existing customers why they bought your stuff won't help solve this mystery. At best, they'll tell you how it just "felt right" without giving you any valuable details as to what that means exactly.

Are they being difficult when they don't tell you the reasons why they buy? Or is something else happening here, where even their best efforts to recall the decision process simply doesn't tell us anything useful? Why won't they just reveal their inner process to you?

Sometimes, it may be that they don't want to share that with you, but research tells us that most often, they really don't know.

Choosing is an emotional and often irrational process.

Asking someone *why* he or she bought can be similar to asking why they fell in love with a particular person. Sure, they can give you all the details of the relationship or the things they like about that person, but we know these decisions are made through emotions, not analysis. Therefore, these reasons are not what truly compelled them to fall in love — or to buy.

So if people can't tell you *why* they made a choice, don't waste your time asking them.

For example, one of the key reasons people buy is because they believe they *should* have the product. Other people have it, and so should they. This illogical herd mentality is rooted in our insecurities about making a decision that others will judge as negative. They want the "right" choice!

The Power of Focus

In its simplest form, *Uniqueing Your Brand* leverages the power to *focus*. And there is no faster way to lose focus and weaken your brand than to extend your identity into multiple categories. The narrower you state your focus, the more powerful it is in the minds of the consumer because they want to choose *one right thing!*

Dedication to a single focus can be very convincing in informing a customer that you have a superior product as well. After all, if that's all you do, you must be the best, right?

What is the real reason that AUBs make such a strong impression in the minds of consumers? Primarily it's because the specialist can focus on one product, one benefit, and one message.

The more you lose focus, the more vulnerable you become.

This focus enables the marketer to put a sharp point on the message that quickly drives it into the mind. The specialist also has the ability to be perceived as the expert or the best in the market. Generalists must live with that "jack-of-all-trades, master of none" identity.

Changing Is Harder

Trying to get people to make up their minds is hard. You know what is even harder? Trying to get them to *change* their minds.

One of my favorite quotes on this topic comes from John Kenneth Galbraith, who once said, "Faced with the choice between changing one's mind and proving there is no need to do so, almost everyone gets busy on the proof."

Why is it so hard for us to change our minds? Many sociologists speculate it's because we are so confident of what we *already* know that any new information is disruptive and suspect. In general, people would rather be *sure* than correct. I mentioned this in earlier chapters as *anchoring*.

Ultimately, this irrational thought process tells us that *facts* have no real place in the process of consumer decision making.

Luckily, authenticity is a great replacement for facts in the mind.

If customers can feel connected to you and your business through your transparent authenticity when they first encounter your brand, it doesn't matter if you really are the most talented service or valuable product around.

It only matters that they felt something *familiar* in your brand identity—something that related to them on a personal level—and, therefore, you became the best and surest choice.

Element 302: Influence

Celebrity no longer equals influence.

Decades before every celebrity began pimping any product that could afford his or her daily rate, a world-famous film and stage actor named Laurence Olivier

(the one married to Vivien Leigh, of *Gone with the Wind* fame) chose to break the glass wall between movies and TV by acting in a Polaroid SX-70 instant camera commercial.

(View it here: **http://youtu.be/eDB9Ty3WPBc**)

This simple act of starring in a TV commercial sent shock waves through the industry, and while no one really believed that "Larry O" used such a pedestrian device as a Polaroid Instamatic camera to capture snapshots while he and the grandkids were running around Disneyland, the influence of his celebrity was so huge that the commercial ran for years, driving Polaroid sales to previously unseen heights.

It also catapulted what would become a tsunami of celebrity endorsements, now spanning millions of media hours over decades of success.

Personal Trumps Social

One thing we did gain with the advent of the Internet is the ability to seek "expert endorsement" from someone whose *experience* is specialized and relevant, even if that person is not local or previously known. This *trust leader* influences us to a better purchase decision.

And we are now even beginning to see "social endorsements," where people we have some personal connection with give us advice or recommendations instead of strangers on review sites like Yelp or Angie's List. These social connections are gaining ground and success as **influencers** (i.e., people who value themselves for being "in the know") have embraced this more intimate form of evangelism.

Except for a very few market makers, like Oprah, the days of celebrity being synonymous with influence are behind us. Now you'll need more than Paris Hilton or the Kardashians endorsing you or your product to find real success in the minds of your prospects — unless you're actually selling celebrity, of course.

So how well is your current marketing message working for you? Not great? Maybe that's because you're not memorable enough.

Pioneers in scientific memory research postulated many years ago that people forget about 80 percent of what they've learned within twenty-four hours of encountering information. And their research subjects were students who had every intention of retaining as much as possible of what they learned.

How much of your four-paragraph life story do you think is actually sticking in the heads of disinterested potential prospects? I'm betting zero percent.

By sticking with the power of AUBs, you can overcome this lack of stickiness, because it enables people to connect from the inside out by reminding or informing them of your purpose and emotional values.

Element 303: Discounting

Price reductions intended to attract clients that otherwise would have ignored you is a failure.

Marketing legend David Ogilvy once said, "Any damn fool can put on a deal, but it takes genius, faith and perseverance to create a brand" (Ogilvy, 1986).

Entrepreneurs increasingly dilute their own brands by relying heavily on discounts and promotional campaigns.

Instead of focusing on how they can over deliver to their customers or outperform their competitors, entrepreneurs often get lost in the short-term revenue buzz that comes from discounting opportunities like Groupon.

This has proven to be the road to ruin for many small businesses. (And, ultimately I believe the same will happen to Groupon, itself.)

The Groupon Failure

The Groupon *promise* is that by offering deeply discounted services or products, you will attract prospects that would have otherwise not noticed you. Nonsense. I believe that the vast majority of these new prospects didn't notice you for good reason; they didn't really want to pay for you in the first place.

Or worse, recent evidence shows us that these great deals are being snapped up by customers who are already long term or loyal. Either way, these types of deep-discount community-based coupon systems are really just cannibalization in disguise.

In essence, they're convincing you to cut off your leg, sell it for half what it is really worth, and then give 50 percent off that price. Groupon-like models are a bargainer's dream and a small-business nightmare.

The bottom line on promotions like these is that the more you direct your clients' focus toward deals and discounts, the more you distract them from your true brand value and dilute your message. This destroys any unique value you ever possessed to begin with.

Unless you've got Walmart's deep pockets and enormous head start in the heartland of America, price can't really be used to define your AUB difference.

By definition, being better *must* be worth more in the minds of the consumer. It's ultimately the reason for making the case that your customer should be paying more for your product or service.

One way to resolve this price-as-differentiator dilemma may be to remove the terms *price* and *quality* from our vocabularies. Instead, replace the term *price* with *exclusive* and *quality* with *unique*. Here are a few basic rules of thumbs for these types of offerings.

1) Prestige products must cost more because people expect to pay more for an elite product. No one trusts the authenticity of Tiffany earrings on sale at a swap meet.
2) Any high-value message a customer is willing to pay a premium for must be *seen* as valuable by their friends and their social connections. No one removes the brand symbol from a $250,000 Mercedes Benz sports car, not even Jay-Z.
3) All top-of-the-market products and services must offer some form of prestige branding. For example, flashing a black American Express card elevates my social status.

This brings us back to the primary "why buy?" questions that consumers ask, like "How can I benefit from what you offer? How are you better? How are you different from the others?"

If your answer in any way ties back to your price-performance ratio, then you are already on the downside of your company's lifecycle. (For those new to the phrase "price-performance ratio," it's an MBA term that just means you're selling what you have as cheaply as you can.)

Discounting is an excellent example of doing something that feels good in the moment but ultimately will not make you or your business happy.

On the other hand, as celebrated business-book author Jack Trout warned us about in his book *The Power of Simplicity*, "If you're not different, you'd better have a low price" (Trout and Rivkin, 2001).

Personally, I can't think of anything more unsuccessful than that.

Element 304: Progress

Activity doesn't equal progress.
(If you're on the wrong path, being in a hurry only makes it worse.)

If you are putting in sixteen-hour days, five to six days a week and it isn't to keep up with customer demand, *stop!*

Your business is not growing, so *stop* doing whatever you're doing right away!

Do something else. Do *anything* else!

Because what you *are* doing is clearly not working. But you already knew that. Didn't you?

Many entrepreneurs confuse activity with progress, sometimes even intentionally. They figure as long as the wheels are turning, they must be going somewhere; they never acknowledge or admit that their wheels don't yet reach the ground.

Alternately, it's equally as bad to have your wheels on the ground and be focused on roaring quickly onward but have no real direction or goal for where you want to end up. I'm not sure which is worse — spinning your wheels or speeding away in the wrong direction.

Ironically, small businesses have the least amount of disposable resources and cash and yet are often models of inefficiency and waste. That's not because entrepreneurs aren't smart. It's because they confuse activity with progress.

Flying versus Not Falling

In the beginning, there was you, your product, and your potential market. The three of you then jumped off the entrepreneurial cliff and entered the free-fall world of small business. *Surviving* was now your primary goal. This basically meant trying to slow the fall and avoiding a fiery collision with the ground.

So how did you survive and keep from crashing?

If you are like 99 percent of start-up entrepreneurs, getting paid for anything close to your mission was the most effective way to slow that drop, sometimes even stopping your fall completely for a little while.

It didn't really matter what you got paid to do or build; you just knew that making money meant you weren't crashing—at that moment. After a while, you may have gotten good enough at surviving that you couldn't even see the ground anymore. Congratulations, you've stopped *falling*. Now what?

Successful businesses must do more than *not fall*.

They must learn to climb higher, turn quickly, and go faster when needed. That's flying. Flying and falling have very little in common, even though they may look similar from the ground.

So before you can learn to fly, you must realize that you have to stop trying to *not fall*. (Bear with me, here.)

This can be tough because it's all you've likely known how to do since you started your business. It may even be the only thing you can be sure you're good at. Make no mistake, though; ultimately, if all you do is focus on not falling, you will never succeed in flying or in business.

If you don't break away from that *survival* mind-set, your business will slowly and inevitably slip into the mists and disappear, taking your hard work, resources, time, and amazing potential with it. Success is about growing your wings by flapping.

OK, so what do you need to do to fly? Mostly, you have to learn to *embrace risk*; knowing that you may have to risk what you've just built to achieve the next goal. If you are not willing to do that, then don't fool yourself into thinking that you can fly.

I know this is a scary landscape, but all successful entrepreneurs will tell you that they risked losing it all more than once. Being tenacious about learning to fly is critical. Once you've reconciled that in your mind, then you need to engineer efficiency into your business.

The less time you spend avoiding the crash, the more time you can spend focusing on where you want to fly and how to get there.

Activity versus Progress

Spending all day putting out fires doesn't make you a successful businessperson unless your business is fighting fires. I wouldn't be surprised to discover the word *entrepreneur* originated as some obscure translation meaning "perpetually short on time, money, and resources."

So how *should* you spend your day?

The first rule of efficiency is to spend *all* of your time doing stuff that only *you* can do. This often means outsourcing things like the physical delivery of your product(s) or service(s) so that so the balance of your time and focus can be best spent on finding more customers.

The time you spend on things that can be outsourced is like a tiny bit of poison in your daily meals. It'll eat away at your available resources (time, money, focus) and kill you so slowly that you may not notice until it's too late. But kill you it will.

Following the legendary advice of Peter Drucker will help you down the path to success: "Do what you do best, and outsource the rest" (Drucker, 2010). Live it or die.

Element 305: Selling

Unsophisticated selling has been replaced by sophisticated buying.

I have had many discussions with small businesses that are starving because they haven't learned how to find and catch fish effectively, metaphorically speaking.

These conversations seem to break down into two categories:

1) Fish finding
2) Fish catching

The topic of finding fish is, by far, the most complex and difficult to define. In contrast, fish catching is both simpler to master and immediately valuable to the survival of your new and/or growing business.

Why? Partly because, with the help of social-networking sites, sales opportunities are likely presenting themselves to you every day.

Sure, there may not be as many as you'd like, but that only makes your ability to catch the ones swimming into your personal space that much more important, right? (Additionally, how frustrating would it be to have a big school of yummy fish in front of you and not know how to catch them?)

But now you're saying to yourself, "If it's easy to learn, what's stopping every small-business owner from becoming an effective salesperson, especially when the product is *you*?" The answer may surprise you. It doesn't feel right. And that's because the action is named poorly.

It shouldn't be called *selling*. It should be called *buying*.

That simple change in terminology makes the sales process a lot easier to understand for everyone involved in the relationship. Rather than the openly aggressive (and possibly even hostile) concept of making someone do what *you* want them to do, we can now see it from a more empathetic and partnering position—that is, helping them define what *they* want to do—in this case, *buy*.

Sounds too simple to be true? It's not.

In fact, for hundreds of years, the most successful salespeople have been using techniques that reinforce them as advocates for the buyer rather than for the seller. They consistently outperform colleagues trying to "sell" the same products.

Consider this from your personal perspective as a consumer. We all like to *buy* stuff, right? But who among us likes to be sold to?

Selling to an Unsophisticated Client

So how is it possible that one business can demand $1,000 for a service or product and clients line up around the block, while others are lucky to get a tenth of that price or lead response? Can there really be such a difference in how they make their products? The secret of quality tells us that can't be true. So, where does the difference lie?

As demonstrated, the perceived value of your business lives primarily in the performance of the service, not just in the results produced. By *performance*, I don't just mean being nice and doing what you said you'd do without drama. This is what any respectable entrepreneur does while delivering a service.

In the earlier examples of both Jennifer Rozenbaum and Charlie the Whistling Plumber, their *performance* included everything that went into creating a valuable experience, from unclogging a drain to the in-tune whistle to a personal epiphany that comes from an empathetic conversation.

This seems like common sense, doesn't it? Yet I repeatedly encounter businesses that insist that their value comes directly from how they *make* their products and strive to *educate* their clients to their inherent value.

For example, they may believe that increasing the number of business awards or recommendations posted on their website enables them to explain why they are so much more valuable to the prospective client.

Fail.

Let's change context and see if it matters. How would you like it if your car mechanic insisted on explaining the intricacies of a BMW fuel injector and how complex they are to adjust and understand and why that makes him worth the extra money to fix your car?

Fail.

OK, so how about my favorite example category, the professional photographer? Would you like your photographer to explain that the real difference between *art* and everything else (she shoots *art*, of course) is in the correct composition and depth of field that only someone with her fifteen years of experience can capture?

Double Fail. These efforts all fail for one simple reason.

You are selling a sophisticated product (you) to an unsophisticated customer (them).

The customer has no real desire or need to understand a higher-than-everyone-else's price argument. The solution isn't in teaching them how to value what you know; it is to understand what *they* value.

And what they value about YOU is **authenticity**.

A Transformation Story: Me Ra Koh

I first met Jeff in 2004 when he gave me the opportunity to speak at a business conference he had created. It was my first speaking engagement in over two years. Before this, I was a published author and speaker at women-centered events. I had written a book called *Beauty Restored: Finding Life and Hope after Date Rape*. The book was based on my own story of how I pieced my life back together after being date-raped in college.

Beauty Restored was released the same day my daughter was born. When she was three months old, we hit the road and did a two-year book tour with speaking engagements in numerous cities. I loved seeing hope ignite in the eyes of women when they realized they were not alone in their pain. Sharing my story and seeing the healing that it brought to women were what I wanted to do with the rest of my life. Enter Jeff the business coach and his idea about Authentically Unique Brands. Our business grew. A lot.

Then there came a turning of the tide, resulting mostly from a shift inside me. I couldn't shake this growing desire to somehow get back to directly empowering women instead of just pursuing a lucrative career as a product spokesperson and presenter.

By this time, my husband, Brian, had left his secure six-figure high-tech job to help build my media business, which had also become our bread and butter. I wondered if there was a way to still do that—so we could keep food on the table and pay the bills—and empower women, specifically moms, at the same time.

This is when my arguments began with Jeff and when I truly experienced the incredible frustration that many of his students also know firsthand. (I eloquently phrase these as "Damn it, Jeff!" moments.) Using the tenets of *Uniqueing Your Brand*, he *challenged* Brian and me to rethink our commitment to our existing business because it seemed so clear that the time to embrace *who I am and what I'm about* was *now*.

"Not falling is not the same as flying, Me Ra," he'd say.

The risk felt too great; we had a family to provide for. We had an award-winning photography business that averaged $20,000 per project in fees. Heck, even Sony had honored me by hiring me as a product evangelist. Wasn't there a way to do both? Couldn't I change the world and still do our bread-and-butter business on the side? Was choosing one—and only one—focus that vital?

Yes, it was.

"Choosing is hard," Jeff would say, "and, sadly for you, people can't remember two messages." I argued. I cried. I tried everything to prove him wrong. And in the end, Brian and I knew that we had to set a path for the next season and prepare for what was still ahead.

In 2010, Brian and I made the commitment and jumped. Following a particularly brutal three days at a Uniqueing Your Brand workshop, we walked out with a new mission plan.

We would use cameras and photography to help moms grow confidence while we created a safe place that allows for healing.

Our business goal had evolved into "get in front of every mom in America," and one of our key strategies was to get me on TV, as an expert in both photography and "mom-ness." We all knew that building strong, authentic partnerships with global companies could help make this happen. We also knew that our old "season" was over.

It didn't matter that Brian and I had no idea of how to make a TV show, let alone get me on TV as a guest. No matter what we chose, we faced mountains that seem too high to climb. Yet as we got clearer about our purpose — increasingly able to declare our authentically unique brand(AUB) — the world responded. Just as Jeff said they would.

I told Sony our new focus and braced myself for what I assumed would be negative frustration. Instead, they embraced the clarity and shift in our mission and leaned in to help us reach more moms.

I'd been pitching Oprah's producers for two years — each rejection teaching me more about what they needed. Then, one day, one of her producers called. Oprah was going to launch a new daily show on NBC centered on her favorite interior designer, Nate Berkus. "Can you tell me what you're about?" asked the producer.

"Why, yes!" I thought. "Thanks to my AUB. I can tell you in one sentence!" My mission was so clear that the producer felt instant confirmation in flying me out to interview for the spot of Nate Berkus's go-to photo expert on his daily NBC show.

All of a sudden, I had gone from not knowing much about TV to spending two years talking to two million moms who needed help making time and emotional space for their families. After the show wasn't picked up for year three, Disney was so pleased at what we had accomplished with those millions of moms that they invited Brian and me to meet with them about another huge project.

And unsurprisingly, one of the first questions from a Disney VP was, "Can you tell me what your mission and business goal are?" *Yes!*

I have found that my clarity and consistency in answering this question — without hesitation — has been vital to partnering with other successful people and companies. Being able to declare my AUB, which reveals my authentic passion, let Disney know right away that our missions were aligned. Six months later, we began filming my first TV show for the Disney Junior channel, *Capture Your Story with Me Ra Koh*.

Since then, the world has never stopped pulling us forward, and we have successfully launched our family series, *Adventures with Me Ra Koh*, into global distribution. The world is rewarding us for knowing who we are, who we want to be, and our purpose for all of it.

I'm in awe of how *Uniqueing Your Brand* has enabled our business to grow and evolve so effectively. Brian has gone from shooting alongside me to being a director and co-producer for Sony, Target, and Disney. (He loves being the director because he finally gets to boss me around.) Without question, Brian and I are working happily now.

Sure, we've come to accept that there are no guarantees. Risk is essential and unavoidable. Every leap we make is still scary. But as we practice flapping our wings, we feel those wings getting stronger. Instead of being afraid of falling — and crashing — we are in love with flying.

Next Steps

There are only a few businesses in any market that are able to just do what they want. And the reason they have this freedom is because they've developed a clientele and a business model (with very high pricing) that allows them to be choosy. Now that can include you and your business.

Congratulations!

The Cult of You

My personal goal for every businessperson I work with is for him or her to discover how to work happily, and do it for the rest of his or her lives. *Uniqueing Your Brand* is the most effective and proven way I've ever discovered to do that.

By determining what actually makes you happy (not just what feels good) and then building a clear and authentic message and business model around that goal, you will transform from who you are today into whom you want to be tomorrow.

Achieving this transformation is the *self-actualization* I keep referring to, and it lives at the top of the "happiness pyramid" defined by Maslow, and broadly accepted by the psychological community. The journey to self-actualization (where you become an even better *you*) has a powerful effect on how you see yourself and how the world sees you.

Before you roll your eyes at my flowery ideals, remember that this is a business book, not some new-age feel-good piece. For me, achieving self-actualization is at the core of creating long-lasting, profitable business models.

Self-actualization will attract like-minded others to you as customers, advocates, evangelists, and, ultimately, true believers. Once this is accomplished, you will have successfully created a "Cult of You."

The essence to making an Authentically Unique Brand work for your business is that it, and you, *must* stand for something so that your *who* becomes your primary differentiator and the real value of your business.

There is a sense of ultimate well-being when you've successfully specialized. For example, you may finally realize that you are good enough, because the root of most personal insecurities (e.g., comparison) ceases to be relevant.

As I explained in the "Brand Value" section, since there is no competition in the market of *you*, as a *person*, there is no true competition against you as a creative- or personal-service business either.

No matter how big or small your local market is, only you can be the best example of you for your client. This is one of the most difficult concepts to embrace and also one of the most important if you expect to succeed as a specialist.

Generalists will continue to seek out customers who will pay them to *do* something (e.g., pose that kid, schmooze that client, or lift that bale). *Uniqueing Your Brand* works and succeeds *only* with businesses that have or want to have a clientele and a business model (with very high pricing) that allow them to be exclusive.

That's where specialists must strive to flourish. Specialists must want to be specialists and aim for the top of their market pyramids, with all of the risk, work, and rewards that come with that decision.

Creating Your Own Love Potion

Uniqueing Your Brand isn't meant to be a cookbook as much as an encyclopedia of (previously secret) ingredients and their effects on people's behaviors. Its purpose is to enlighten you to the presence of these elements and the powerful effect they have on business successes and profitability, so you can act with more knowledge and intent in your business strategies and marketing efforts. That doesn't mean that this book is academic. In fact, the information and suggestions associated with each element is meant to give you the insights and direction you need to be able to apply this to your success.

One way to put all this valuable information immediately to work is by approaching each major section as steps forward. Starting with Section 1, you can follow the execution advice contained in those five chapters (e.g. define your Authenticity Words) to create the basis of your own authentically unique brand identity. Section 2 (Brand Value) will guide you through the process of ensuring your message is as effective as possible. Section 3 (Brand Execution) is full of advice on how to get your new AUB message into the hearts and minds of that *perfect customer prospect* that you will have worked so hard to identify and target.

By using all fifteen chapters as your core recipe guide—and careful application of their instructions at each stage—you will find that at the completion of this Uniqueing Your Brand process you will have successfully turned lead into gold and created your own love potion formula.

The Real Secret Ingredient

Of course, as in many things of this nature, the devil is in the details and once you've created and launched your AUB you feel that you aren't getting the response you believe is possible from the love potion that you've created... don't be afraid to start again. Sometimes it takes a few iterations to get really good at cooking up the potion that produces the *exact* magical effect you desire. Just the act of repeating your efforts will make you faster and more productive.

Sure, sometimes you get lucky on the first try (I did on company #3) and sometimes, it takes a bit longer and tests your fortitude (company #1 for me took six different formula creations before I found the right one.)

To help you get it right, I'll pass on the same advice I got, and that I restate to myself in the mirror more frequently than you know...

Trust in yourself.

Trust in the process.

Trust in the result.

Authenticity is the (not so) secret ingredient to your success.

Every business or entrepreneur who I have worked with or monitored that has embraced this Uniqueing Your Brand process has found awe inspiring levels of success and happiness, with a handful of rare exceptions (out of thousands of successes) that were inevitably tied either to a complete change of business direction or simple lack of focused determination.

If you want the kind of amazing results that come from building your brand based on your authentic self, you need only dedicate yourself to following these secrets and relentlessly pursue those customers that will make you happy... and rich.

To help you along in this pursuit, I have also put together a series of additional tools (videos, webinars, homework, and anything new I can think of to help you achieve the success levels I know are possible with this system) and you can access them anytime.

http://jeffjochum.com/UYB-extras

For those of you who prefer a more detailed, systematic approach—with specific goal-setting, lesson plans and even homework—I recommend you review the content of the video course I created during the research for this book, referenced in the "On-Demand Education" heading, below.

Some Final Cautions

Uniqueing Your Brand isn't an ad campaign, sales promotion, or this year's marketing fad. It won't work if you approach it as something you will try out and see if it sticks. It's a very real commitment to define the personal AUB of your business and your purpose and let it change your life.

A successful specialism business must remain specialized. Once you reach that comfortable plateau, diversification is destructive; if you chase other business ideas it will erode your validity as a specialist in the minds of your customers. For example, brain surgeons didn't diversify when facelifts suddenly became popular.

Ironically, most entrepreneurs initially reject the general idea of being locked into one focus or specialty. They want to do as many things as they can, thinking that diversity increases their chance to succeed.

After all, that is what the big companies do, right? What many entrepreneurs don't realize is that every time they head out to be something else, they open the door for another company to become the specialist, taking the market they've built away from them.

This doesn't happen overnight by one upstart competitor, which makes it even harder to see coming. It happens as a result of many specialists each taking a small piece of your business until you bleed out. Death by a thousand cuts.

Uniqueing Your Brand is about focus, not sacrifice, and reaching a point where you are empowered to say no to clients who simply don't fit your *who*. Specializing in one thing often means you must give up some of your generalist bread-and-butter business, knowing the more success you have specializing, the less general business you'll attract.

On-Demand Education

Uniqueing Your Brand is the result of three years of research in the area of specialism and unique branding. During that time, I created a video course (titled "Specialism Brand Essentials") for the purpose of teaching and testing many of the concepts expressed in this book. Until this book, I've offered them only to my private students, as part of my one-on-one coaching program. I am now happy to make them available to you, as well. You can access them at the link below.

http://jeffjochum.com/SBE

Online Communities

I've also started a community devoted to the creation, practice, and advancement of AUBs on Facebook. This group is open to all and brings together a tight, loyal collective of overachieving businesses who don't want to be part of the pack and are compelled to be leaders, mentors, and influencers in their industries. This is your invitation! The group can be found at the following URL:

http://facebook.com/groups/specialism

Work with Me

If you'd like to take AUB and specialism to the next level for your business, and want some help doing it, let's talk. For more information about my coaching and consulting options, visit my website:

http://jeffjochum.com/consulting

Acknowledgments

So many people to thank! The rest of the book is finished and ready for printing... this chapter is a testament to the intimidating blank page that must tell everyone who helped me get this book in your hands how absolutely important they are.

Let's start with my wife, Mary Ellen (aka Mel) and my two youngest kids, David and Nicholas. They have been incredibly patient with dad's late nights, early mornings and locked office doors for over a year. While I am truly satisfied from the process of researching and writing this book, I do look forward to having "extra" time to spend with them, once again. Add to that the wonderful support I get from my Mom (Marie) and my older kids Holly and Savannah, and I'm neck-deep in the loving thoughts.

That leads me to the next ring of my family circle; there are six special entrepreneurs I've worked with and coached over the last decade who have created companies that change lives and make millions happy: Thanks for always generously including me in your lives and endeavors, as well as your amazing insights, Me Ra Koh & Brian Tausend, David Jay & Todd Watson, and Garrett Delph & Jared Bauman.

I'm also silly proud of the students who've grown into sought-after mentors and coaches in their own rights: Jennifer Chaney, Christine Tremoulet, Stephanie Ostermann, Jane Ammon, Michelle Lehman Ocampo, Leeann Marie Golish, Ivona Kaczmarek-Dixon, Jennifer Goldberg Rozenbaum, Brian Friedman, Sarah Roshan, Sarah Lehberger, Tracy Moore, Jackie Haugen, Jason & Maggie Henriques, Meg Wise, Tori Pintar, Stephanie Moore-Milne, Meghan Thomas, and (especially) Jason Groupp. I love you guys more than you can know.

Next, a huge shout-out to my top-of-the-class students who've integrated the science of specialism wonderfully into their own businesses: Ali Anderson, Ali Brannan, Alicia Hanson Sturdy, Alyssa Andrews, Alyssa Turner, Amanda Lamb, Ananda Paulas, Andrew Barlow, Angie Johnston, April Amodeo, Ashleigh Victoria, Aubrey Hord, Audrey Michel, Barrett Ross, Beckie Brockie, Ben & Britney Higgs, Brandon Chesbro, Brittany Smith, Brooke Summer, Carmen Salazar, Carrie Swails, Casie Zalud, Cassandra Bradley, Charisse Rhodes, Chelsi Clark-Supinski, Cherri Hong (Me Ra's mom), Chris Loring, Chris Scott, Christy Arias, Cindy Harter, Colson Griffith, Daphne Chan, David Mendoza III, Devon Knudson, Dylan Burr, Effie McCormick, Elmer Platzer, Emily CH, Emily Jean Smith, Erica Rose, Erica Swanteck, Everett Stout, Frank Donnino, Gregory Byerline, Hannah Hardaway, Heather Richardson, Heidi Morgan, Hillary Shemin, Jacque Jones, Jacque Vue, Jaime DiOrio, James Christianson, Jasen Arias, Jason & Gina Grubb, Jason Lackey, Jason Toevs, Jeff Lundstrom, Jelger & Tanya, Jen Lightful, Jen Snyder, Jenelle Kappe, Jenessa Evans, Jenni Owens Lillie, Jennie Crate, Jessica Dragosz, Jessica Haley, Jessica Ulrich, Joey Chandler, Joleen Vincent, Julie Anne Neill, Julie Renee Massie, Julie Templin, Julie Watts, Justine Russo, Kain Tietzel, Kaitlin Cooper, Kamran Zohoori, Kate Loose, Kathi Cook, Kathryn Andrews, Katie Lyon, Katrina Meyer, Kaushlesh Biyani, Keith Pitts, Keri Vaca, Kevin Sturm, Kim Campo Hartz, Kim Harrison Nodurft, Kim Rodgers, Krisd Mauga, Kristi Chelgren Meinhardt, Kristina Marshall, Lauren Dahn, Linda Viglione, Lisa Novitsky, Lori Kennedy, Mandie Haberman, Maria Fuller, Matthew & Amy Coppersmith, Matthew & Courtney Cotter, Matthew Tan, Megan Bookhammer, Meghann Byerline, Melanie Soleil, Melissa Hirsch, Melissa Mullins, Meredith Harris, Merissa Lambert, Mick Shah, Michelle Gardella, Mike Colon, Mike Larson, Mike Peysner, Nat Valik,

Nicole Dolan, Nicole Nichols, Paige Puglisi, Pearl White, Pete & Emily Haack, Rachel Abelson, Rachel Aberle, Rachel Avery Conley, Rachel Schrepel, Raquel Bowles, Regas Kefalonitis, Regina Mountjoy, Rodney Bedsole, Ruben Parra, Samantha Sinsel, Sara Hasstedt, Sara Monika, Sara Sankiewitz, Sarah Nelson Garcia Conklin, Sarah Zimmer, Savannah Chandler, Scott Courtney, Scott Lawrence, Sean & Mel McLellan, Seshu, Sharon Arnoldi, Shira Zimmerman, Sonja Spaetzel, Steven Dahn, Susannah Allen, Tanja Aelbrecht, Tanja Butler Melone, Terra Cooper, Tess Pierson, Tessie Reveliotis, Tim Halberg, Tina Mahina, TJ Romero, Tracy Somerville, Trisha Casey, Tyler Bertrand, and Vickie McConnell.

Finally, there is everyone I can recall who have helped me in the specialism community, focus groups, and on Facebook (and I typed in every name myself!): Airika Pope, Alawode Oluwasegun, Alex Beadon, Alexander Rubin, Ali Anderson, Allison Cordner, Amanda Bedell, Amanda Deibel, Amanda Kopp, Amber Reinink, Amber Tyler, Amy Bartley, Amy Bartley, Amy Pezzicara, Anabelle Perez, Andrea Catlett, Andrea Golod, Andrew Singh, Angelique Cox, Angie Brinkerhoff, Ann-Marie Walker Keeney, Aous Poules, Ashleigh Thompson, Autumn Cutaia, Beau Peterson, Bill Gellerman, Brian Joseph Calabrese, Briana Rickman, Brianna Dunn, Brianna Hall, Brissa del Mar, Brittany Rogers-Hanson, Bryan Caporicci, Caitlyn Bom, Calin Ardeleanu, Candice Cunningham, Carrie Kizuka, Casi Lark, Cassandra An Daniel, Catherine Bliss, Catherine Hall, Cathy Nance, Chad DiBassio, Charla Avery, Cherene Watkins, Cheryl O'Neil, Cheryl Spriggs, Chris Creed, Chris Humphreys, Chris Mortensen, Chris Stark, Chris Szulwach, Christa Maull, Christie Sodon-O'Connor, Christine DeAngelis, Christine Garza, Christopher John, Claudia Johnstone,

Colin Breece, Craig Swanson, Cristie Rosling, Crystal Garner, Cathy Mores, Cynthia Olkie, Cynthia Phillip, Dalisa DeChiara, Dana Parns, Dave Hein, David Apuzzo, David Quisenberry, Dawn Kitley, Dawn Matheny McCarthy, Deb Houske Schrobilgen, Denie Burridge, Denise Saucedo, Dennis Rodgers, Derek Decrane, Dianna Schisser, Douglas Clarke, Elizabeth Haase, Elizabeth Langford, Enna Grazier, Eric Bellamy, Erin Cady, Ezra Ekman, Felelcia Stovers, Femke Muntz, Grace Suphamark, Greg Moss, Gavin Wade, Hanssie Ho, Heather Anita, Heather Bowman, Heather Sedrick, Heidi Jons, Heidi Moellmann, Hilda Holmes, Ho Yin Au, Ieva Geneviciene, Jackie Hogue, Jaleel King, James Milnes, James Shepard, Jamie Swanson, Jamin Scherz, Jamye Chrisman, Janna Curran, Jared Wilson, Jason Beaver, Jean Huang, Jefferson Pals, Jeffrey Cruz, Jeffrey Shipley, Jen Vanderby, Jeni Buchanan, Jenna Walker, Jenni Heffner, Jennifer Bunt Becker, Jennifer Dunn Wilson, Jennifer Johnson, Jennifer Rapoza, Jennifer Tallerco, Jennifer Winder, Jenny Cheasman, Jessica Cudzilo, Jessica Lark, Jessica Vallecorsa, Jill Velazquez, Jim & Katrina Garner, Joan Reynolds, Jodi Oosterlee, Joe Maull, Joel Llacar, John Pace, John Wills, Jonathon Ellul, Jose Malave, Julie Ferneau, Julie Foskett, Julie Patton, Julie Sawatsky, Julie Story, Julie Templin, Julie Whaley, Kafi D'Ambrosi, Kaitlynn Connelly, Karen ReVelle, Karie Denny, Karin Griffin, Karlo Gesner, Karrie Sheinker, Kate Oman, Katie Osborne, Katie Schoepflin, Kelly Cowleson, Kelly Jo Spurlock, Kelsey Bigelow, Kelsey Schweickhart, Kendra Ellis, Kim Lewis, Kimo Holmes, Kris Walters, Krystal Woods, Lara Eastvold, Laraine Mullaney, Larry Sovinski, Laura Shortt, Laurie Bracewell, Leah Nicole Roberts, Lesley Notton, Linda Grennan, Lindsay Long, Lucia Ruiz, Lydia Santiago Gillis, Lynsi Piar, Magdaleen Kemp-Pretorius, Mandy Leigh, Margret Larned, Maria Alcantar, Marietta St Onge, Mary Hurlbut, Mary Louise

Delano, Nathaniel Kim, Matt Grazier, Matt Kennedy, Matt Meiers, Matt Thompson, Matthew Johns, Meghan Walker MacAskill, Megan Sells, Meghan Robles, Melissa Albert, Melissa Mazza, Melissa Mullins, Merari Biancucci, Merari Zaldana, Michel Guindon, Michelle Touchetter, Micole Pettit, Mindy Joy Rose, Miqui Miller, Mirranda Reinhardt, Mitch Arnett, Nancy Marie, Nathaniel Fuents, Nicole Conner, Nicole McClung-Ridella, Nikka MacDonald, Okema Clare, Oscar Setiawan, Paige Elizabeth, Pam Hutchins, Patricia Penta, Paul Retherford, Paul Schatzkin, Peggy Farren, Peter Dylg, Rachel King, ReBecca FreeBurn, Rebekah Dorn Budziszewski, Regina Young, Regis Hervagault, Renee Steinmann, Rhema Peterson, Ricardo Antonio Rodriguez III, Rob Goldstein, Rob Nicholson, Robyn Kilponen, Rochel French Vos, Rose Pierce, Sandra Halvatzis, Sara Hull, Sarah Hendee, Sarah Lillard, Sarah Ulrich, Scott Kretschmann, Scott Shaw, Scott Williams, Scott Wyden Kivowitz, Shannon Adelson, Shannon Worgan, Shauna Stanyer, Sheila Buhr, Sheryle Lynne, Sofi Seck, Sona Sood, Stacie Frazier, Stacie Kurt Jensen, Steph Zh, Stephanie Tadlock, Stephanie Tetreault, Steve Mohr, Svetlana Yanova, Syed Yaqeen, Tamara Christy, Tammy Snyder, Tara Reiners, Taryn Chrapkowski, Terence Law, Teresa Klostermann, Teri Shevy, Thomas Campbell, Thomas Morelli, Tiffany Heidenthal, Tim Elliott, Tim Marman, Tina Joiner, Todd Thiele, Tonja Peterson-Wendt, Tracy Woodger-Broz, Travis Broxton, Trish Casey, Twyla Wisecup, Vanessa Joy, Vanessa Robinson, Wayne Masut, Wendy Poole, Yolanda Pucinski, Yusaf Gunawan, and Zeus Martinez.

Lastly, I want to thank the incredible editing and technical teams at YouBeYou Books and Amazon's CreateSpace for turning a writer's death-march into a labor of love. You guys make me want to write another book… maybe next year. ☺

About the Author

Jeff Jochum is a serial entrepreneur, best-selling author, internationally respected speaker, and marketing scientist.

Over the last thirty years, he has written four business books; founded, bootstrapped, and sold three of his own companies; and licensed products to Computer Associates, Borland, and Microsoft.

He was instrumental in the creation of the hosted business website market when, in 1997, he co-founded **EBZ.com** — creator and publisher of **e-Biz in a Box**, the world's first best-selling DIY website design product for small businesses — a company he sold for a substantial return three months before the dot-com bubble popped.

After that bullet-dodging success, he spectacularly failed at getting onto the PGA's Senior Golf Tour, succeeded as CEO for two business *turnarounds*, and failed at a third. He then served time as an Angel Capitalist; investing in a few online startups to better-than-average results before realizing he is happier making money than investing it.

Following that epiphany, he returned to the hands-on world of marketing and sales, leading the teams at **Pictage.com** to over $40 million in revenues in less than two years (acquired by equity giant Apax Ventures) before serving as Chief Marketing Officer at web superstars **DeviantART** and **SmugMug**.

In 2010, he "retired" and began working exclusively with innovative start-ups and creative entrepreneurs, coaching them to success using the secrets found in this book.

Feel free to contact him at **jeff@jochum.com**.

Bibliography

Ariely, D. 2010. *Predictably Irrational, Revised and Expanded Edition: The Hidden Forces That Shape Our Decisions.* HarperCollins.

Briggs, R., and G. Stuart. 2006. *What Sticks: Why Most Advertising Fails and How to Guarantee Yours Succeeds.* Kaplan Publishing. Kindle Edition.

Brown, B. 2012. *Daring Greatly: How the Courage to Be Vulnerable Transforms the Way We Live, Love, Parent, and Lead.* Penguin Group US. Kindle Edition.

BusinessDictionary.com. January 2016. "Meaning of Commoditization." http://www.businessdictionary.com/definition/commoditization.html.

Dawar, N. 2013. "Tilt: Shifting Your Strategy from Products to Customers." *Harvard Business Review.*

Dictionary.com. November 2015. "authentic." http://dictionary.reference.com/browse/authentic.

Dictionary.com. November 2015. "perfect." http://dictionary.reference.com/browse/perfect?s=t.

Dictionary.com. November 2015. "unique." http://dictionary.reference.com/browse/unique?s=t.

Drucker, P. 2010. "A New Way to Outsource (Kate Vitasek)." *Forbes.com*, June 1. http://www.forbes.com/2010/06/01/vested-outsourcing-microsoft-intel-leadership-managing-kate-vitasek.html.

Einstein, A. January 2016. "Einstein Quotes." Brainy Quote. http://www.brainyquote.com/quotes/quotes/a/alberteins121993.html.

Fields, W. (Performer). 1939. *You Can't Cheat an Honest Man.* (movie)

Galbraith, J. K. December 2015. BrainyQuote. http://www.brainyquote.com/quotes/quotes/j/johnkennet109909.html.

Godin, S. 2009. "define: brand." *Seth Godin's Blog.* http://sethgodin.typepad.com/seths_blog/2009/12/define-brand.html.

Honeywill, R., and C. Norton. 2012. *One Hundred Thirteen Million Markets of One.* Fingerprint Strategies Inc. Kindle Edition.

Jobs, S. 1998. *Business Week*, May 25.

Ogilvy, David 1986. "New York City luncheon." Quoted in Lipman, G. *The Race to Zero: Time to Rethink 'Discount' Mentality.* HuffingtonPost.com (Jan. 15, 2015)

Pascal, B. 1658. *The Mystery of Jesuitisme by Blaise Pascal, [Translated into English], Second Edition Corrected, Page 292, Letter 16: Postscript, [Letter addressed to Reverend Fathers from Blaise Pascal].* London: Richard Royston.

Pelling, M. 1981. "Barbers and barber-surgeons: an occupational group in an English provincial town, 1550–1640." *Bulletin of the History of Medicine* 28:14–16.

Rapaille, C. 2006. *The Culture Code.* Broadway Books.

Reichheld, F., and T. Teal. 1996. *The Loyalty Effect.* Harvard Business Press.

Ries, A., and J. Trout. 2009. *The 22 Immutable Laws of Marketing: Exposed and Explained by the World's Two (Kindle Location 534).* Harper Collins, Inc. Kindle Edition.
Shaw, G. B. 1903. "Maxims for Revolutionists." *Man and Superman.*
Simonson, I., and E. Rosen. 2004. *Absolute Value: What really Influences Customers in the Age of (Nearly) Perfect Information.* HarperCollins. Kindle Edition.
Trout, J., and S. Rivkin. 2001. *The Power of Simplicity.* McGraw Hill Professional.
Twain, M. 1897. Note to anonymous. Quoted by twainquotes.com.
http://www.twainquotes.com/Death.html.
Twain, M. 1871. Mark Twain to James Redpath, June 15. Elmira, New York. *UCCL 00617 (Union Catalog of Clemens Letters).*

30508404R00114

Made in the USA
Middletown, DE
27 March 2016